HOW TO FACE IAS INTERVIEW

CHARACTER AND NATION BUILDING

HOW TO FACE IAS INTERVIEW

CHARACTER AND NATION BUILDING

DR. B. RAMASWAMY
MR. VISHNU BHAGWAN
PROF. DR. G. BHASKARAN

PRABHAT EXAMS

Publisher

PRABHAT EXAMS

Imprint of Prabhat Prakashan Pvt. Ltd.

4/19 Asaf Ali Road, New Delhi–110 002

Ph. 23289555 • 23289666 • 23289777 • Helpline/ 7827007777

e-mail: prabhatbooks@gmail.com • Website: www.prabhatexam.com

Edition

2025

Price

Four Hundred Seventy Five Rupees

ISBN 978-93-5266-684-3

Printed at

Sita Fine Arts, Delhi

HOW TO FACE IAS INTERVIEW: CHARACTER AND NATION BUILDING

by Dr. B. Ramaswamy, Mr. Vishnu Bhagwan, Prof. Dr. G. Bhaskaran

ISBN 978-93-5266-684-3

₹ 475.00

Preface

All IAS aspirants know that the preparation for the IAS/IPS Interview is no single day affair, it is a continuous process. Logically, the candidate should keep the interview session in mind the day he starts preparing for the prelims and a clear focus, in addition to a proper schedule, are required along with proper planning. Reading of relevant books, journals and newspapers needs to be undertaken in a routine fashion by every IAS aspirant. They need not discontinue with this habit before the interview. They should also improve their conversational skills with the right pronunciation. They should start discussing with experienced colleagues about what they read to enhance their conversational skills. The candidates should also make a self-analysis of their strengths and weaknesses and make a conscious effort to play on their strengths. The candidates need to understand in black and white that the personality test for the highest civilian job is a test not only for intelligence and knowledge but also quality assessment of overall personality, attentiveness, leadership abilities and balance of judgment, honesty and integrity that are required for an administrative post of the highest order.

This book tells readers all about UPSC IAS interviews, including the important tips for cracking IAS/IPS interview. The sample actual questions asked at UPSC interview are given along with sample tough IAS toppers personal interview questions and answers. The various types of questions asked at the UPSC interview are explained. Sample model tricky questions asked in IAS examination are given. All-important interview skills required to clear IAS / IPS interview are described. The most recommended approach and framework for UPSC interview preparation are prescribed. The importance of understanding the phenomenon & process of IAS/IPS interview, along with the roles of communication skills, body language, time management and stress management are given. Also, the role of character and decision-making in preparing for personality test at an IAS interview are critically evaluated. A detailed point-wise presentation of guidelines to face IAS interview is highlighted. The importance of knowing some do's and don'ts at IAS interview is analyzed. The answer to question like, how to perform better in IAS interview, is given. The significance of inculcating interview skills among candidates is described in brief. In addition, the tips to boost interview skills, are presented. Also, the best way to prepare for civil services interview and giving proper answers to interview questions, are discussed. The importance of knowing the interview structure and the ways to communicate effectively in interview are given. The candidates are made to understand the fact that an interview practice makes one perfect and a proper strategy / tactics for handling a panel interview are must for a solid performance. Knowledge is imparted regarding the questions to expect at the IAS interview and the commonly asked potential interview questions. The important clues for UPSC interview are given. The significance of keeping the right attitude in UPSC's IAS interview and the significance of hobby and motivation in IAS interview are narrated. The reason why to become civil servants is explained in detail. The most important tips to prepare for civil services examination is given and the five good reasons to opt for civil services as a career is recommended. Ways to keep the best mindset while preparing for civil services interview is suggested.

This book also creates an understanding of interview in its totality. Knowing the types of interviews, the importance of interview, mock interview and bio-data/curriculum vitae is described. The significance of an informational interview is explained and the ways to handle group discussion and interviews are given. Also, the stages in personality development are described with focus on tackling personality based interview questions. Some important tips for the IAS personality test are discussed, such as, remembering some important topics at IAS interview; model IAS interview questions; inculcating the best ways to prepare for IAS interview; best test of the personality of an IAS interview candidate and model probable questions asked mostly in the IAS interview. This book also inculcates proper learning ways to improve skills at IAS interview. A sample 'out of the box' questions asked in IAS interviews are given with focus on sample IAS interview; and model IAS toppers' answers. A concluding overview of IAS interview is also given, so as to enlighten candidates about the ways to excel.

Authors

About the Authors

Dr. B. Ramaswamy is a well-known social scientist, educator, author & motivator. Till recently, he was Pro-Vice Chancellor of APG Shimla University, Shimla, Himachal Pradesh. Currently, he is Legal Advisor to Members of Parliament. He is Member, Divisional Railway Users' Consultative Committee (DRUCC) on Railways of Chennai Division, Govt of India. He is Visiting Member to the Centre of IT and Social Science, Indraprastha Institute of Information Technology (IIIT). Member, Doctoral Advisory Committee, Indraprastha Institute of Information Technology (IIIT) Delhi. It is a research-oriented university. Academic Advisor, Bon Secours College for Women, Tanjore (TN) (A Grade by NAAC) affiliated to Bharathidasan University.

He has obtained all his qualifications from the reputed institutions and universities such as Loyola College, Delhi School of Economics, etc. Apart from his exemplary achievements in the field of sociology academically and professionally, he has several other qualifications and professional achievements in the fields of Disaster Management, Journalism and Mass Communication, Human Rights, IPR, Cyber Law, Personnel Management, Industrial Relations, Vedic Culture, Leadership, Women and Children, Disability Studies etc. He holds a Doctorate in Sociology from Singhania University, Honorary Doctorate from Cosmopolitan University, USA & Inter-American University of Humanistic Studies, Florida, USA in the field of Social Science. He was also awarded Honorary Doctorate in Humanities by Apostolic International University, affiliated with and accredited by International Institute of Church Management Inc., USA. He has guided M.Phil and Ph.D scholars in various areas. He is a Visiting Fellow, Advisor, Member in several

About the Authors

Dr. B. Ramaswamy is a well-known social scientist, educator, author & motivator. Till recently, he was Pro-Vice Chancellor of APG Shimla University, Shimla, Himachal Pradesh. Currently, he is Legal Advisor to Members of Parliament. He is Member, Divisional Railway Users' Consultative Committee (DRUCC) on Railways of Chennai Division, Govt of India. He is Visiting Member to the Centre of IT and Social Science, Indraprastha Institute of Information Technology (IIIT). Member, Doctoral Advisory Committee, Indraprastha Institute of Information Technology (IIIT) Delhi. It is a research-oriented university. Academic Advisor, Bon Secours College for Women, Tanjore (TN) (A Grade by NAAC) affiliated to the Bharathidasan University.

He has obtained all his qualifications from the reputed institutions and universities such as Loyola College, Delhi School of Economics, etc. Apart from his exemplary achievements in the field of sociology, academically and professionally, he has several other qualifications and professional achievements in the fields of Disaster Management, Journalism and Mass Communication, Human Rights, IPR, Cyber Law, Personnel Management and Industrial Relations, Vedic Culture, Leadership, Issues of Women and Children, Disability Studies etc. He holds a Doctorate in Sociology from Singhania University, Honorary Doctorate from Cosmopolitan University, USA, & Inter-American University of Humanistic Studies, Florida, USA, in the field of Social Science. He was also awarded Honorary Doctorate on Humanities in Apostolic International University, affiliated with and accredited by International Institute of Church Management Inc., Florida, USA. He has guided M. Phil. and Ph. D. scholars on his competent areas. He is a Visiting Fellow, Advisor, Member in several prestigious institutions both in government and private such as IIT Roorkee, YASHADA, Raj Bhawan, Pune and NIPCCD, Govt. of India, Delhi. He has published more than 250 articles/books both in national and international magazines/publication of repute.

He continues to write articles to leading magazines and newspapers. Being a renowned social scientist, he is an invited speaker to deliver key note addresses and chief guest to various functions, seminars, national and international conferences, convocations and workshops. He travelled to more than 19 countries to deliver various areas of lectures. He motivates large number of youth including the school children. He makes tremendous impact while delivering each lecture which brings tremendous mind transformation to the youth of India towards nation building. He holds important positions in Government viz Member, Maintenance Tribunal, Maintenance and Welfare of Parents and Senior Citizen Act 2007. He also worked as Deputy Chief Warden, Civil Defence Corps, Delhi and as Director in very many institutions and private bodies. He was an acting Chairperson, Child Welfare Committee, Government of NCT, Delhi–A bench of Magistrates constituted under section 29 of Juvenile Justice. Being an expert social scientist and educationist, he is interviewed regularly by the various electronic media, TV channels and Press. His passion is directed towards our nation building through quality education especially to those who are deprived of quality education. He has so far produced more than over 1000 civil service officers in the country.

Mr. Vishnu Bhagwan, IAS, retired as a Chief Secretary in Haryana Govt. Worked as Head of Civil Service in the State. Apart from functioning as Secretary of the State Cabinet, he coordinated activities of all the departments.

His educational background have been B.A. (Hons.) Economics, St. Stephen's, Delhi Uni. M.A. Economics, Delhi School of Economics, Delhi Uni. L.L.B., Law Faculty of Law, Delhi Uni. M.Phil, Public Admn., Indian Institute of Public Administration, Punjab Uni.

He worked as Principal Secretary to the Chief Minister of Haryana, as Principal Staff Officer with the Chief Minister assisting him in day disposal of work as well as policy formulation also functioned during the period as Secretary of the Departments of Civil Aviation, Public Relations, Vigilance and Grievances. He was Chairman of Haryana State Industrial Development Corporation, and Haryana State Electronics Development Corporation. Financial Commissioner & Secretary, Education & Languages Deptt. Planning and Administration of education in the entire State of Haryana from Primary to University level and including Adult Literacy Programme.

Financial Commissioner & Secretary, Irrigation & Power, Excise & Taxation Departments. Administration of these important departments at the State level. Was responsible for planning and introduction of structural reforms in the Power Sector for bringing about improvements in efficiency and viability in generation, transmission and distribution of power in the State. Was also responsible for supervision and implementation of Water Resources Rehabilitation and Consolidation Project sanctioned by the World Bank for the State.

Minister Agriculture and Deputy Permanent Representative of India to FAO and Allied Organizations in Embassy of India at Rome. Represented India in the meeting of FAO and Allied

UN Bodies at Rome. Was member of FAO Council, Programme Committee of FAO, Governing Council of WFP, during the entire stay. Chaired the Group of 77, Rome Chapter and served as a co-coordinator of Asia Group.

He was posted as Deputy Commissioner, Sonepat & Faridabad State of Haryana. Director, Ministry of Tourism and Civil Aviation Government of India. Joint Secretary, Ministry of Agriculture, Dairy Development Government of India. Commissioner and Secretary, Irrigation and Power State of Haryana. Commissioner and Secretary, Food and Civil Supplies Department, State of Haryana. Resident Commissioner, Haryana Government at Delhi. Joint Secretary, Ministry of Agriculture Policy Planning, Govt. of India.

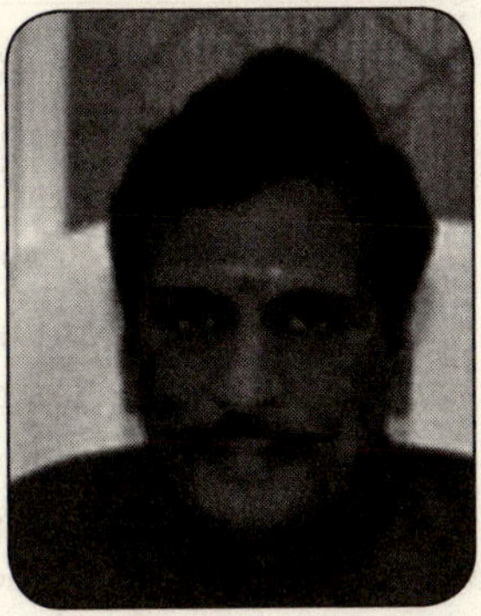

Prof. Dr. Bhaskaran, the internationally well known personality who experiments Indian culture and human values with the paradigm of Philosophy, is presently the Vice Chancellor of Tamil University, Thanjavur, Tamil Nadu, a unique institution that preserves the tradition of culture, art and literary values of classical Tamil language with research, teaching and cultural innovations. He has specialized in the field of Culture and Philosophy.

His hard work and dedication has many visionary aspects in introducing Yoga at University level in the early 1990's in Teaching, Research and Practice in Tamil Nadu. Teaching the inner meanings of Saiva and Vaishnava concepts with human values. Spreading the values of Yoga in foreign Universities with an inspiration from our Hon'ble Prime Minister, Shri Narendra Modiji. Giving motivational talks to students and young scholars on achieving goal with Religion, Ethics and Culture. Coordinating scholarly discussions on Hindu Philosophy involving various mutts and Religious Heads, etc., 28 Seminars and Conferences, both National and International, organized by Prof. Dr. G. Bhaskaran are well crafted with scholarly papers with the participation of internationally acclaimed scholars on various subjects, dealing with Yoga, Culture, Philosophy and humanism. This scholarly achievement created academic space for Philosophical interaction.

Member, Board of Studies in Saiva Siddhanta, University of Madras. Member, Board of Studies in Philosophy, University of Madras. Member, Board of Studies in Jainology, University of Madras. Member, Board of Studies in Philosophy (PG), Pondicherry Central University, Pondicherry. Member, Board of Studies in Philosophy (UG), Pondicherry Central University, Pondicherry. Member, Board of Studies in Indian Culture, Govt. Arts College (Men) Autonomous, Kumbakonam. Member, Board of Studies in Philosophy and Culture (UG), Bharathidasan University,

Tiruchirappalli. Member, Board of Studies in Philosophy & Culture (PG), Bharathidasan University, Tiruchirappalli. Chairman/Member, Board of Examiners, University of Madras, Madurai Kamaraj University, Bharathidasan University, Pondicherry Central University, Calicut University, Usmania University, Kuppam Dravidian University. External Expert in Jaffna University, Sri Lanka to evaluate the university teachers for their promotion and also Member of Board of Examiners for M.Phil. and Ph.D. Member, Ethical Committee, Siddha Research Centre, Sastra Universty, Thanjavur, 2005. Member, U.G.C. Minor Project Selection Committee, 2006. Nodal Officer, U.G.C. Selection Committee for the development of Humanities and Social Sciences Research Programmes in Colleges, 2006. Member, Faculty of Arts, Annamalai University, 2007-2010. Member, Board of Examiners, UPSC, TNPSC. Member, Board of Examiners, UGC's NET. Member, Board of Examiners, SLET.

Contents

1

How to Face IAS Interview: Character of Nation Building

Character is the quality that makes a person or a group of persons different from others. It distinguishes the good from the bad. It underscores the fundamental features of strong and weak men in their bid to make a clear statement in life. Character is the seed of life.

At this time in our national life, it is necessary to cross-examine some of the ideals which have shaped the very character of the Indian state. Whether there are good or bad, right or wrong, strong or weak, or even desperate or sublime.

The character of its leaders has shaped the Indian state over the years. From the colonial to post-independence India, those who have ruled or governed the nation have entrenched an innate character in the life and history of the country.

The one thing we must appreciate is that character is the only factor that is constant in leadership, just as change is a permanent feature of any process, be it political, economic, social or industrial development. A leader can pass away but his character remains a mirror to history's admirers because it is a reference point in succeeding leaders' actions and inactions.

Another important thing is that character is the beauty of life. To live a good life, one must decorate it with an exemplary character worthy of emulation.

Nation Building

India has now been gifted, with a young population. If the youth are taught to develop their cognitive intelligence to become original thinkers; imbibe emotional intelligence to develop team spirit and a rational risk-taking attitude; inculcate moral intelligence to blend their personal ambitions with national goals; cultivate social intelligence to defend civic rights of the weak, defend gender equality, and develop the courage to fight injustice; and develop spiritual intelligence, then India can develop a superior species of human beings—youth who can be relied on to contribute to making the country a global power within the next two decades. For this we have to work on three fronts.

The first front is ability empowerment—the development of the seven types of intelligence (emotional, social, moral, spiritual, environmental, and innovational).

The second is a collective mindset about the legacy and future of the nation, which means knowing the correct defalsified history of India.

The third is the commitment to a social contract of rights and obligations such as a fundamental right to quality primary and secondary education, right to work, an obligation to compete for most positions of employment on merit, practice gender equality and place national interests above selfish interests.

A national policy for integrating spiritual values and organisation leadership can be achieved through measures by which we can create a modern mindset among the youth.

This will not only motivate them to acquire technical cognitive competence, but also develop their emotional, moral, social, spiritual, environmental and innovational intelligence.

This will make them patriotic, self-reliant individuals of high character, possessing a social conscience. Governance, business ethics and organisational leadership haveto be founded on that pool of talent.

The Prime Minister's Vision of New India

"I invoke Team India to run for a New India by 2022. By then the poor shall have concrete houses, the farmer shall double his income, youths and women will get ample opportunities, an India free of casteism, terrorism, corruption."The Prime Minister Narendra Modi.

The Prime Minister of India, during his Independence Day address, laid out his vision of a New India where the youth of our nation become key stakeholders in building the India of the 21st century.

He underscored the fact that we are a nation of young people; the children born at the dawn of this century will come of age in 2018. Thus, it is clear that for New India to be a developed nation, it has to be powered by its most valuable resource: the bright, educated youth who are highly skilled and are capable of being job creators.

How to Face the IAS Interview?

IAS interview is a half-an-hour exercise that can change your life, the nation's and people's life. A high score in UPSC interview can sometimes create a difference of more than 100 marks with fellow candidates in just under 30 minutes. Being the last round, this would give one an unassailable lead in the competition. Though the final rank list is prepared by taking the sum of UPSC mains marks and interview marks, very often we see that interview highscorers top the final selection list too.

AVERAGE MARKS OF SELECTED CANDIDATES IN CIVIL SERVICES WRITTEN EXAM & INTERVIEW

	2012			2013			2014			2015		
	Candidates Selected	Average marks in Written	Average marks in Interview	Candidates Selected	Average marks in Written	Average marks in Interview	Candidates Selected	Average marks in Written	Average marks in Interview	Candidates Selected	Average marks in Written	Average marks in Interview
General	457	786	191	517	629	180	590	739	177	499	729	171
OBC	295	775	179	326	607	169	354	708	171	314	698	165
SC	169	724	171	187	586	167	194	697	167	176	681	163
ST	77	740	180	92	572	168	98	676	170	89	672	162

The nature of personality test for the Civil Services Examination is different from those of the other services interviews. The candidates aspiring for Civil Services are going to be interviewed by a board already aware of their personal as well professional track record.

They are questioned on matters of general subjects, related to national and international importance.

The motive of the interview is to assess the personality of the candidate for a career in public service by a board of competent and unbiased observers who themselves having excellent career profile as a bureaucrat under different capacities with years of experience in public services.

The test is intended to judge the mental strength of a candidate. In broad terms, this is really an assessment of not only his intellectual abilities but also social traits and his curiosity in day-to-day happenings of national and global importance. Some of the qualities to be judged are mental alertness and strength, critical analysis and assimilation, clarity in thoughts and logical exposition, balance of judgments, diversity and depth of interests, ability for social cohesion and leadership qualities, intellectual and moral integrity, patriotism and interest for service of the nation etc.

Candidates should have an interest not only in their academic subjects but also in the events which are happening around them both within and outside their own state or country as well as in modern currents of thought and in new discoveries.

So here, one is required to be diplomatic in taking up a stand and tackling the issues in given circumstances. The precision of language, discipline of thought and lot of patience in placing the views are the prerequisites. Remember, your entire personality is going to be judged on every single word to be spoken there. Thus, one needs to be extra careful about selection of words while being interviewed.

DO's

❖ Develop Character of Nation Building

Character of youth is very important for the nation building; develop your character in the path of national leaders such as Gandhi and Nehru. Imbibe characters such as truth, ahimsa or love, control of the palate, non-stealing, non-fearlessness, removal of untouchability, bread labour, tolerance, equality, communal unity, respect of religions, sawdeshi.

❖ Be an Early Bird

Don't waste time in waiting for Mains Exam results, which only leads to stress and frustration and instead start early preparation. Start polishing your personality as early as possible.

❖ Knowing Ourselves

The most crucial problem with us is that we don't know ourselves fully. A human being has so many shades, covering the depths of the hearts. We know so many things, but we don't know ourselves. Try to know the different aspects of your personality, open, hidden or unknown. If any of your personality traits does not suit the character of nation building, try to overcome them.

❖ Cultivate a Good Body Language

Work on your body posture, personal appearance, and body language, as you are going to be judged on the basis of this in the interview. During the interview, keep yourself calm, maintain eye contact, listen to the panel members very patiently, greet them well and appear very attentive yet with a composed body posture.

❖ Be an Optimist

There are many myths and rumours about IAS interview. You might have bad experiences from previous interviews as well. But don't let negative thoughts to ruin your confidence. Don't waste energy and time on matters – interview board, position, questions etc. – which are beyond your control. Hope for the best.

❖ Work on Your Confidence Level

Everyone loves people with self-confidence so appear confident in front of the panel members. If you are unsure about an answer, don't get nervous, just say that you don't know. You cannot have the knowledge about everything under the sun, so it's very normal. Just feel relaxed. If you are sure about your beliefs, answers or solutions, express them confidently. But remember the line between confidence and over confidence; just be confident but don't cross the line.

❖ Improve Your Communication Skills

Improve your communication skills for UPSC interview. If you search for words in the 25 to 30 minutes UPSC personality test, you may run short of time to express your ideas completely. Listening to debates and news on television channels is one practical way to improve communication skills. Also, start talking with your friends in the medium for UPSC interview.

❖ Read Your DAF Thoroughly

Most of the questions in the UPSC interview will be based on your detailed application form (DAF). Read your DAF thoroughly several times and prepare well for the questions from the areas such as education, hobbies, past work experience, services preference, etc.

❖ Develop Problem-Solving Skills

Problem-solving skills are relevant for evolving solutions to a problem or set of problems. A problem is a gap between desired state of affair and actual state of affair at a particular point of time.

In order to overcome this gap, relevant action is required. For identifying this action, problem-solving skills are required. Problem-solving skills are relevant for solving the daily problems of people as public servants.

❖ Straight to the Point

Master the art of giving to-the-point answers. Very often, long answers can be condensed into crisp, but interesting statements. Don't beat around the bush.

❖ Be up to Date with Current Affairs and Read the Newspapers Thoroughly

Keep yourself aware of the important current news, elections, government policies, etc. Read Economic Surveys, Yojana, Kurukshetra and the Indian Year book thoroughly and take notes from them. The panel may ask you about the news that appeared last week and also previous day in the newspaper, so keep yourself updated. Make sure you revise the current affairs of the past one month.

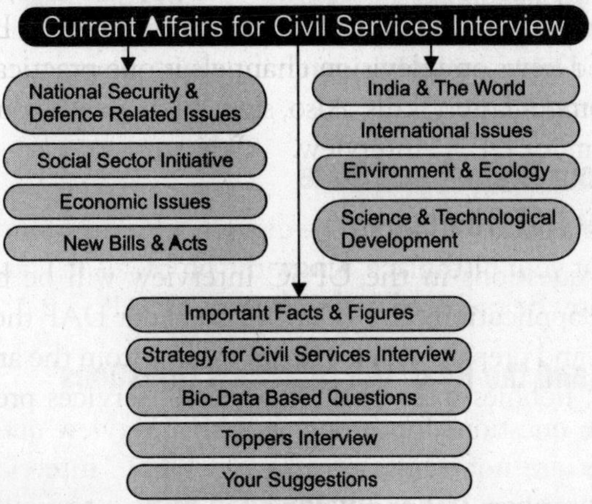

❖ Strengthen Your Optional Subject

It is seen that many candidates tend to neglect their optional subject after UPSC CSE Mains. But UPSC interview panel may ask questions from your optional subject at the interview. Brush up recent happenings related to your optional subject, focus on current affairs related to your optional.

❖ Prepare Well on Your Hobbies

Very often, this is the first question UPSC interview board ask, many times in a light mood. Make sure you start well. Don't give cliché answers. Hobbies help the interviewer to understand the personalities of candidates. Keep practicing your hobbies until the last week before UPSC interview and also gather some knowledge on your hobbies.

❖ Go Through Your Graduation Textbooks

UPSC expects candidates to take their graduation seriously. As this is one area where the interview panel perceives the candidates to have expertise with. So, more in-depth questions can come from this area.

❖ Learn to Give Balanced Judgements

Your views should be balanced and impartial. This does not mean that you should not take a stand. Ideally, you should have stand – without any political or social biases. Once you take a stand on controversial topics, be prepared with your justification for the same. Don't give sweeping generalizations or particularizations without a proper base.

❖ Know Your District and State

Questions may be asked about the district, region and state. Collect details about your birthplace. Know the problems in your village or city and state. Be prepared with solutions as well.

❖ Understand the Real 'IAS Interview Questions'

Most of the questions forwarded as 'IAS interview questions' on the internet are not questions asked in UPSC interview. UPSC says 'The interview test is not intended to be a test either of the specialised or general knowledge of the candidates which has been already tested through their written papers'. Read IAS UPSC toppers interview section to know about real UPSC interview experience.

❖ Apply Commonsense

Many people who are good at knowledge sometimes miss the commonsense, so commonsense is also an important part of interview. Sometimes UPSC members ask questions which can be answered just by using commonsense. But the stress on the interview day may hamper your thinking process. Realise that commonsense is not common. Expect some puzzles which require on-the-spot critical or lateral thinking.

❖ Neat and Clean Attire

The first impression matters. But it is not necessary to wear expensive blazers or suits for UPSC interview. Be comfortable with what you wear. For gents, a light-coloured shirt and dark trousers should give a professional appearance. A simple churidar or saree is recommended for ladies. Whatever you wear, in that dress you should look confident and neat. Avoid going with stylish haircuts and beards because after all we are not going for modelling but for public service.

❖ Be Polite

It is better that you remain polite throughout the interview process. Even if any unpleasant situation is created by an interviewer (this may be done deliberately to test your patience), do not lose your temper. If you lose your temper to protect your ego, you may be treated as a highly emotional person. Remember, these personality traits are not considered suitable for any job. If you are polite in the interview, it conveys that you have respect for other's perspective; you are open-minded to accept new ideas and change yourself accordingly, as per the demands of a given situation. All these will go in your favour.

❖ Re-check Your Documents

We advise to carefully verify the documents before going to interview to avoid last-minute panic. Ensure that you have all necessary documents ready.

❖ Practice Standard Questions

While preparing for examination, some students adopt the practice of writing answers of standard questions to whether they can complete required number of questions within the stipulated time. In the light of this practice, they try to overcome their deficiency if there is any. In the same way, you can practice standard questions likely to be asked in the interview. This process will give you confidence as you will be able to eliminate any deficiency that you experience during this process.

❖ Reflect Prime Minister's Idea of New India in Your Answers and Thoughts

It is always important for the interview candidate to have a strong knowledge on the present government's aspirations and policies, so it is advised to read about the prime minister's aspiration of New India by 2022.

❖ Be Yourself

Don't try to present before UPSC board a fake personality. Don't mug up ready-made answers for UPSC interview. Be yourself and express your opinion.

❖ Enrol for Mock Interview

Make sure to attend atleast 3 to 4 mock interviews and improve your preparation based on the feedback by panel experts before appearing for the final UPSC interview. The basic objective of a mock interview is to give an interviewee feeling of an actual interview. This feeling emerges because the mock interview is conducted on similar conditions or creating the similar environment to that of the UPSC.

❖ Evaluating Mock Interviews

After the mock interview is over, it is essential that its result is evaluated so that deficiency, if any, is overcome. While evaluating the result of mock interview, treat it as real interview. The result should be evaluated by yourself as well as by the interviewers. It is better that first you evaluate your own performance in the mock interview and subsequently ask feedbacks from the interviewers.

Don'ts

❖ Don't Take UPSC Interview in a Lighter Way

Be serious about the process and questions. Give respect to the board members who take your personality test. Never underestimate the persons in the board. They have vast experience and knowledge. Don't be too casual on serious questions.

❖ Don't Lie or Fake

Don't say lies to impress UPSC interview board. Never create fake facts in your bio-data. Very often they will catch you.

❖ Don't Stop Reading Newspapers

Candidates often stop reading newspapers once the UPSC main exam is over. However, information about current happenings is very important for IAS interview, just like the UPSC main exam.

❖ Don't Compromise Your Moral Integrity

UPSC not only measures one's intellectual qualities but also social traits and values. Ensure that your moral integrity is sound.

❖ Don't Be Swayed by Rumours

Many UPSC candidates are seen to be carried about by the rumours about the personality test. Certain boards are seen tight in awarding marks while others are perceived as liberal. Though slight variations may come, in reality, all boards award high and low marks depending on the performance of the candidate on the date of UPSC interview.

❖ Don't Repeat Certain Words Too Frequently

Some interviewees repeat certain words such as 'it is nothing but…, 'I mean that…, 'I feel that…, 'according to me…, etc. repeating such words quite frequently by an interviewee during the interview process creates bad impressions in the mind of the interviewers. Therefore, try to avoid uttering such words beyond the required proposition.

❖ Don't Hesitate

Many interviewees show hesitation during the interview process. In the interview process, an interviewer may ask a question which has not been understood by the interviewee correctly or not understood at all. In such a case, the interviewee should request the interviewer to repeat the question but the interviewee fails to do so out of hesitation. Result, either he gives wrong answer or shows his ignorance about the answer. Both these options go against the interviewee.

❖ Do Not Take Your Cell Phone inside the Interview Room

If you have to carry it inside the interview room, keep it in off position. Ringing of a cell phone distracts attention, which is not liked by anyone and may be considered, in all probability, as offensive by those aged person.

❖ Do Not Speak about Your Qualities Too Much

Let your qualities speak about you themselves. If you happen to speak about your qualities too much, it will raise expectations of the interviewers and they would evaluate you against those raised expectations which can prove disastrous for you at the end, and it is not fair also.

Some Other Don'ts

Do not show nervousness during the interview process. Do some exercise/yoga/meditation to overcome your nervousness before the interview.

Do not make any adverse comment on the facilities provided or about the mode of communication to the UPSC etc. during any point in the interview process, remember all these are secondary stuff.

Do not check time by looking at your wrist watch during the interview process. This is a sign of low confidence.

Do not show any type of fidgetiness even if your interview is not proceeding on the line of your expectation. Try to bring the situation back according to your expectation by overcoming those obstacles which has caused this phenomenon/situation and if you cannot, they themselves would do; just keep the patience. They sometimes check your mindfulness and patience during unfavourable and tough times. So take it in that spirit.

Do not show any clue, either verbal or non-verbal, that you are very much desperate for this career. Desperation of any kind is not liked. If you do well in the interview, you will be offered the position.

❖ Useful Books

- *Leadership and Personality Development*, DR. B. Ramaswamy.
- *Crack Civil Services in First Attempt*, Divey Sethi IRS.
- *How to Become an IAS*, Dr. Vijay Agrawal.
- *Imagining India*, Nandan Nilekani.
- *India 2020: A Vision for the New Millennium*, APJ Abdul Kalam.
- *India's Struggle for Independence*
- *India After Gandhi*, R. Guha
- *Character and Nation Building*, M K Gandhi
- *Ethics in Governance Report*

❖ Conclusion

"If I was given six hours to chop a tree, I would spend the first four hours sharpening the axe."Abraham Lincoln

This saying suggests how good interview preparation for exams such as IAS can bring changes in one's life. Your interview session may last for twenty minutes, thirty minutes, or an hour, but you have to prepare yourself for a much longer period.

The personality test assesses one's demeanour and not what a candidate says but how he or she says it. Moreover, the final assessment or marks given to candidates are based on what they have answered and not for the questions that have been unanswered.

UPSC interview in most cases is a friendly exercise. There is not much to fear about, except that your chances of selection depend on it. Be truthful to yourself and answer confidently.

"All the best to all for your UPSC interview."

❑❑❑

2

How to Develop Positive Attitude?

Introduction

"Positive persistence is the key when it comes to overcoming setbacks and odds in life's journey."

Positive thinking is a mental and emotional attitude that focuses on the bright side of life and expects positive result. One of the most important keys to success is positive thinking. With this key, it is easier to achieve success, improve relationships, have better health, and enjoy happiness, satisfaction and inner peace.

This key, also helps in the daily affairs of life, making everything flow more smoothly, and with less friction. This key also requires that you take positive action, since results require both positive thinking and positive action. To use it in your life, you need more than just to be aware of its existence. You need to adopt the attitude of positive thinking in everything you do.

With a positive thinking we experience pleasant and happy feelings. This brings brightness to the eyes, more energy, and happiness. Our whole being broadcasts good will, happiness and success. Even our health is affected in a beneficial way. We walk tall, our voice is more powerful, and our body language shows the way we feel.

How Positive Thinking helps you?

Expecting success and not failure, making you feel inspired, it gives you the strength not to give up, if you encounter obstacles on your way, it makes you look at failure and problems as blessings in disguise, believing in yourself and in your abilities, enables you to show self-esteem and confidence, you look for solutions, instead of dwelling on problems, you see and recognize opportunities.

Benefits of Positive Thinking

It helps you achieve goals and attain success; it brings more happiness in your life; it produces more energy; positive attitude increases your faith in your abilities, and brings hope for a brighter future; you become able to inspire and motivate yourself and others; you encounter fewer obstacles and difficulties in your daily life; You get more respect and love from people; life smiles at you.

The Power of Positive Thinking

Optimists (positive thinkers) seek the valuable lesson in every setback or reversal. Rather than getting upset and blaming someone else for what has happened, they take control over their emotions by saying, "What can I learn from this experience?"

How Positive Attitude Manifests?

Positive attitude manifests in the following ways—Positive thinking, Constructive thinking, Creative thinking, Optimism, Motivation and energy to do things and accomplish goals, an attitude of happiness. If you adopt it as a way of life, it would bring constructive changes in your life, and makes them happier, brighter and more successful. With a positive attitude you see the bright side of life, become optimistic, and expect the best to happen. It is certainly a state of mind that is well worth developing.

Qualities of Positive People

- ***Clarity:*** They keep their minds on what they want, and keep looking for ways to get it. They are clear about goals and they are confident that they will accomplish them, sooner or later.
- ***Looking for goodness:*** Optimists look for the good in every problem or difficulty. When things go wrong, as they often do, they say, "That's good!" And then set about finding something positive about the situation, if you are looking for something good or beneficial in a person or situation, you will always find it. And while you are looking, you will be a more positive and cheerful person.

- ***Positive thinking in action:*** It is easy to be cheerful when everything is going according to plan. But, it is when you encounter unexpected setbacks and difficulties that you demonstrate to yourself, and the world around you, what kind of an attitude you really have. Make sure that it is a positive one!
- ***Positive attitude:*** In order to make positive thinking yield results, you need to develop a positive attitude towards life. A positive attitude makes life look brighter and promising. A positive attitude helps you cope more easily with the daily affairs of life. It brings optimism in your life, and makes it easier to avoid worries and negative thinking.

Examples of Some Positive People

❖ In Civil Services

- ***Ira Singhal:*** Ira Singhal who made history by becoming the first differently abled person to top Civil Services examinations, was earlier denied by the government to join as IRS (Customs and Central Excise), as the service (IRS-C and CE) is not identified "for both the arms affected persons".
- ***Rukhmani Riar:*** After failing class 6 exams in Dalhousie's Sacred Heart School, it is because of her undying passion that she bounced back and became the UPSC all India second topper of the 2011 batch. She cracked the Civil Services exam in her first attempt. She believes that if one decides to persevere and come out of that failure with positiveness, nothing can stop you achieving success.

❖ In Governance

- ***Armstrong Pame:*** Armstrong Pame, an IAS officer from the North-East, has shown exactly what it takes to get things done. His indomitable will spearheaded the construction of a 100 km road without the help of the government.

  He has mobilized children, grown ups and elderly alike to construct a 100 km long road passing through the most backward places in Manipur (including Tousem, the most backward sub-division in Tamenglong district).

- ***Prashanth Nair:*** A 2007 batch IAS officer of Kerala cadre, who has recently been appointed the secretary to the Minister of State for Tourism, Prashanth Nair has earned much public acclaim for kick starting a slew of popular initiatives as the collector of Kozhikode.

  His innovative ideas—such as operation Sulaimani, a decentralized participatory project to address hunger in urban areas; Tere Mere Beach Mein, a project to tackle waste management at Kozhikode Beach; and Yo Appooppa, an attempt to improve the quality of life of the elderly, were huge runaway successes.

  Affectionately called "Collector Bro", Prashanth is also famous for a unique proposal, he had put forward to the people in his district. He offered a free plate of Malabar Biryani to every individual who pitches in to clean a 14-acre pond in Koyilandy. Unsurprisingly, the idea was a resounding success.

❖ **In sanitation**

- ***Maharashtra's Navlewadi village has water, water everywhere and a zillion drops to drink***

  The people of this remote village in Puranya Taluka faced a massive scarcity of clean water. But Modi's Swachh Bharat Mission has encouraged them to battle all odds. The result: A 35,000 litre water tank and several water pipelines have been installed in the village. Thanks to the abundance of water, the village now boasts of clean surroundings.

- ***Thrissur's Puzhakkal village goes from bags to riches***

  Kerala is popularly known as God's Own Country. But rapid industrialization has turned parts of the state into convenient dumping grounds. One such place was Thrissur's Puzhakkal, where solid waste management has always been a major challenge.

However, inspired by Modi's Swachh Bharat campaign, the villagers came together and decided to tackle the piling garbage dumps. They put a proper waste management plan in place. This included removal of waste, installation of waste bins and the setting up of biogas plants. This village has now become a role model for the whole of Kerala.

❖ In Environment Protection

- ***Water man of India:*** Since 1985, Rajendra and his groups have built 4,500 johads, to collect rainwater in some 850 villages in 11 districts in India. This is giving people their livelihood back. The people in these villages now understand how to keep a plentiful supply of groundwater at all times, and if needed how to get more.

  He has been awarded Stockholm Water Prize 2015 and has won a number of awards including the Ramon Magsaysay Award for Community Leadership. But his journey was not as smooth as we can think of. He had to face many obstacles to win the trust of the people and also to overcome all political/ bureaucratic hurdles in a vast country like India.

  His works and achievements are really inspiring to all of us and show us that with the real intention and will force we can do a magic and turn the sides.

- ***Chetla Ramaiah:*** Daripalli Ramaiah (born 1937) is an Indian social worker. He hails from Reddypally village in Khammam district of the state of Telangana. He is the recipient of the Padma Shri Award for the year 2017, for his invaluable contribution to extending tree cover.

  He is locally known as 'Chetla Ramaiah', trees Ramaiah. On a mission to bring back the green cover, he is estimated to have planted more than 10 million saplings in and around Khammam district with a thrust on trees that provide shade, fruit-bearing plants, and Biodiesel plants with assured benefit to future generations.

❖ In Business

- ***KFC:* Colonel Sanders:** At age 5, his father died, begins the story. "At age 16, he quit school. At age 17, he had already lost four jobs. At age 18, he got married. He joined the army and washed out there. At age 20, his wife left him and took their baby. He became a cook in a small cafe and convinced his wife to return home.

  At age 65, he retired. He felt like a failure & decided to commit suicide. He sat writing his will, but instead, he wrote what he would have accomplished with his life & thought about how good of a cook he was. So, he borrowed $87, fried up some chicken using his recipe, went door to door to sell. At age 88, Colonel Sanders, the founder of Kentucky Fried Chicken (KFC) Empire, was a billionaire."

How to Think Positively?

❖ Positive Words

Use only positive words while thinking and while talking. Use words such as, 'I can', 'I am able', 'it is possible', 'it can be done', etc. Allow only feelings of happiness, strength and success into your awareness.

❖ Positive Thoughts

Disregard and ignore negative thoughts. Refuse to think such thoughts, by substituting them with constructive, happy thoughts. Every time a negative thought finds its way into your mind, immediately replace it with a positive thought. In your conversation, use words that bring forth feelings and mental images of strength, happiness and success.

❖ Positive Perception

Before starting with any plan or action, visualize clearly in your mind, its successful outcome. If you visualize with concentration and conviction, you will be amazed at the results. Read at least one page of inspiring book every day. Watch movies that make you feel happy. Associate yourself with people who think positively.

❖ Case Study: Research Experiment

During a research experiment, a marine biologist placed a shark in a large holding tank and then released several small bait fish into the tank. As you would expect, the shark quickly swam around the tank, ate the smaller fish. The biologist then inserted a strong piece of clear fiberglass into the tank as a partition, creating two separate areas. She put the shark in one and put bait in the other.

Again, the shark quickly attacked. This time, however, it only slammed into the divider. Undeterred, it kept trying every few minutes but to no avail. Eventually, about an hour into the experiment, the shark gave up.

This experiment was repeated dozens of times over the next few weeks. Progressively, the shark got less aggressive and made fewer attempts to attack, and eventually got tired and simply stopped attacking.

The biologist then removed the divider, but the shark didn't attack. It had become conditioned to believe a barrier existed between it and the bait fish, so the bait fish swam wherever they wished, free from harm.

Many of us, after experiencing setbacks and failures, emotionally give up and stop trying. Like the shark, we believe that because we were unsuccessful in the past we will always be so. In other words, we continue to see a barrier in our heads, even when no real barrier exists between where we are and where we want to go.

Conclusion

Life is a race that is all about winning. But winning is not the only endpoint. In life, we should understand no one has ever made great achievements on the very first day. In life, we should wait with patience, and just keep giving our best. Hard work pays. So, we shouldn't be disheartened by failures. Life is a long journey and you're the one who is riding the bike on it. If we're passing a rutted road it doesn't mean we'll never face a smooth path. Setbacks are but stepping stones to success.

How many of us have succeeded in what we try in the first attempt? Not many. This proves success cannot be attained in one day. There are exceptions where success can be achieved easily. But when it comes to a competitive task or a tough task, it takes a lot of patience and it needs many attempts to bring success to our side.

Thomas Alva Edison's success story is inspiring. Edison's experiments to refine the light bulb would have failed a thousand times. But his attitude was simply great; he confidently said, I didn't fail 1000 times. I found 1000 ways of how not to make a light bulb.

"Negative attitude says: you cannot achieve success.
Positive attitude says: You can achieve success."

In life, what matters is our positive attitude. If we give up easily, we cannot taste the flavour of success. It takes a year for a tree to give tasty fruits. Similarly, it will take time to make success. If we want to win in life, we should not stop till we finally get what we are looking for.

What will help us mark achievements is self-confidence and positiveness. If we believe we can make wonders, we will. So, we should believe in ourselves before expecting others to believe or support us.

"The pessimist sees difficulty in every opportunity. The optimist sees opportunity in every difficulty—Winston Churchill."

When life gives a thousand reasons to quit, just give yourself one more reason to fight back to build your way to glory. The problem is that we give up after suffering a failure. And we form an imaginary barrier of constant failure in front of us, which doesn't let us to step into the shoes that leads us to success. You'll have to strive hard for it and make yourself believe you can do it — and the imagined mirror of problems will vanish.

❑❑❑

3

How to Keep your Motivation High?

"Life is 10% what happens to you and 90% how you react to it."

Importance of Motivation

Not everyone is born with motivation. There is a severe lack in some who believe 'I'll get to that one day' or 'the timing isn't right' or a classic case of 'I can't do that'. Motivation is the defining factor that turns a good thought into immediate action. It turns a good idea into a business and can positively impact the world around you.

Motivation for Achieving Goals

Goals are the stepping stones towards your dreams. So, in order to achieve them, you need motivation to keep you chugging along towards them. Without motivation, you can't achieve anything. There are no goal posts to aim for and no purpose to strive towards. Motivation is one of the most important factors in determining the level of success that you will achieve. Motivation is required throughout the entire goal process.

Motivation for Purposeful Life

Motivation is an important life skill. The reason is because every person on this earth is unique and has a purpose. To steward your purpose well, you have to be motivated to work towards your goals which helps your dreams become a reality. Not just for your sake, but the sake of others as well.

Motivation for IAS aspirants

During the course of preparation for this exam, many aspirants spend most of their time and energy in daydreaming, hours are spent on imagining various roles you could play to save the imaginary district as DM; or trying to imagine yourself as becoming a celebrity in your village and family, or by topping the exam, in the country.

Dreaming is not a bad thing. But, you should understand that only dreaming without aiming will motivate you momentarily. This sort of motivation fizzles out soon. That is why, you keep on yourself in pseudo-motivation because coming out of that daydream will make you stressful and de-motivated.

To succeed, you need a long-term motivation. Your own actions will prolong the life or death of your motivation, not any dreaming or imagination. Only hardwork and patience will keep you motivated for the long time.

If you are thinking the success story of a topper, or a neighbour, brings you motivation, then you are wrong. You will be motivated for some time but after a night's good sleep or a day or a week, new temptations and new problems dawn upon you, making you less inspired by the story you had read a day before.

Of course, there is no denying the fact that few success stories push you to achieve certain things in life, you will be fired up to achieve the same or better the record. But this only helps you remember your goal. It always doesn't help you get up and get going. So, keep your focus always on your long-term goal and to achieve that set daily goals and finishing them in time will motivate you immensely.

How to Sustain Motivation during your entire Exam Preparation?

❖ Being Independent of Thoughts

You should remove all pressures and imaginations from your head. Become independent completely, from thoughts of making parents happy, revenging the ex-girlfriend/boyfriend, becoming a local celebrity, saving India from the corrupt, and importantly from the thoughts of gaining huge prestige in the society.

Prepare for this exam logically and reality. List the things you want to do today and finish those things. If you are preparing polity today you have to focus only on polity. Not on the day of your exam, question paper or final result where you are giving TV interviews.

❖ Find a Purpose

Yes, you want to be an IAS officer, this is your goal but not your purpose. So, find a purpose like serving society, sacrifice for nation, empathy towards poor, compassion towards animal.

❖ Falling in Love with your Life

Love what you do, love your purpose, love your goal, love reading newspaper, love writing something on what you read, and finally love your life. This will keep you happy and motivated.

❖ Removing Negative Thoughts

When you sit to study, you will face concentration problems like negative thoughts like fear of failure, family issues, stress, imaginary friends etc., when you face these, just sit back relax and pass the thoughts as how the air surrounding you touches and passes on.

❖ Building Motivation Within

Motivation is a muscle that needs to be constantly worked and this can be achieved by reading biographies, enrolling in training and listening to motivational speakers who can share their own successes, while building you up.

❖ Imbibing Values of Constitution in You

Try to imbibe the constitutional values like justice, equality, fraternity, secularism in your daily life which will help you to build you personality because a nation building personality will be always high on motivation.

Following above things have their advantages:

Firstly, as your focus is on today, you will not be demotivated as you will love what you do with a purpose. You will be in reality all the times, expectations will not let you down.

Secondly, it speeds up things for you. You don't have to worry about having less time at your disposal. How? Say, for example, you wrote Prelims, and after 3-4 days of rest, you start following above three principles without worrying about Mains or Interview, by the time, result is announced, you will have finished half the Mains syllabus. This is not unrealistic. It is possible, if you decide to live for today. As you know, tomorrow never dies, the Sun will shine tomorrow, stop worrying about it.

When you start thinking more and more about tomorrow, about succeeding, and about other things the reverse thing happen – you start losing confidence, you will lose motivation and the goal starts appearing distant and move away from you. Your fear make it appear big and insurmountable.

That's why, to keep your motivations high, prepare a small action plan for today and follow it.

Advantages of Motivation

❖ Identifying a Goal

Goals come from a desire to change something in your life. You may be motivated by positive or negative factors. Maybe you are unhappy with some aspects of your life. If this is the case, you would identify what you want instead and set a goal to achieve it. Alternatively, there may be something which you enjoy in life but you would like to experience more of it or, there may be something which you would like to add to your life.

Whether it is a desire for change, a desire to add more or, a desire to add something new, it is motivation for improved circumstances which inspires the goal.

❖ Prioritization

Whatever you want to achieve in life, you will need to commit yourself to it and focus your energy on it. There is only so much that you can do as time and energy are limited resources. As you are constantly inundated with things that you could do, you need to be able to prioritise your activities and focus on the most important tasks. This allows you to achieve your best results. Motivation is critical in helping you to determine which activities should be prioritized.

❖ Action

Anybody can draw up a plan but the value of that plan will never be known until you put it into action. Setting a goal is not enough to achieve it. You need to take consistent, decisive and effective action to bring that goal to reality. The difference between those who consistently take action towards their goals and those who do not, is motivation. There will be days when you don't really want to do anything. On these days, it is your high levels of motivation that will push you through.

❖ Overcoming Setbacks

One of my favourite books is 'The Success Principles (TM): How to Get from Where You Are to Where You Want to Be' by Jack Canfield. In one section of the book, Jack provides a rather amazing statistic. He tells us that 94% of all sales people have given up on the sale after the 4th time of asking but 60% of all sales are made after the 4th time of asking. That means, 94% of sales people miss out on the chance of making the sale because they don't have the motivation to keep asking.

This can be applied to all goals. How many times have you given up on something just because you hit an obstacle? Almost any goal worth achieving is going to require some resilience. You will hit obstacles and when you do, you must decide whether you will continue or give up. Motivation will ensure that you keep going.

❖ Staying the Course

Many of your most important goals will require a great deal of time to accomplish. It is easy to lose motivation and lose sight of your objectives. If you allow this to happen, you may never reach your end goal. It requires a special kind of person to keep their eye on the prize for a long-period of time and, keep taking consistent action towards their goal. What makes these people special is that they are highly motivated and they take action to reinforce their motivation on a regular basis.

❖ Motivation Teaches Perseverance

This ties in with the previous point, but motivation helps you strive through setbacks, trials and fears. Thomas Edison is known for the invention of the light bulb and is noted for this quote, 'I have not failed. I've just found 10,000 ways that won't work.' The famous inventor also inspired this thought, 'Our greatest weakness lies in giving up. The most certain way to succeed is always to try just one more time.' Motivation will teach you to persevere when reality tells you to give up.

❖ Motivation Fights Against Fear

Fear of failure is so common it can literally stop you from taking action. Motivation kicks fear in the butt because it tells it, no matter what I'm feeling, I'm going to do it anyway. Motivated people see beyond their fear and can visualize the outcome. Motivation will always help you see the bigger picture.

❖ Motivation Builds Self-Confidence

When you're motivated to achieve your goal, confidence is a by-product of the little steps taken to see that goal achieved. When you've pushed through setbacks and fear, there is a sense of accomplishment and this builds an inner confidence to try something new. Motivated people will have a few projects on the goals because they have pushed through barriers and seen positive results, which gives them motivation to start new projects and try new things.

❖ Motivation Inspires Others

Motivation is an attractive trait and it can inspire others to make things happen in their own life. If you've ever met or hung out with a self-motivated person, you instantly feel like you can achieve anything because their positivity and can-do attitude elevates your own spirit. Seeking out a motivated person can help elevate your own motivation levels.

Some Success Stories of IAS Toppers

❖ Govind Jaiswal – The Son of a Rickshaw Puller

Born in dismal poverty in Varanasi, Govind achieved 48th rank in 2007's Civil Services results. Govind spent childhood in a rented, congested room that he'd to share with three sisters and his parents, with no scope of time and the right setting for study at all. He began to aspire to become an IAS officer when his father and mother, a rickshaw puller and a housewife respectively, sent him to a school in Varanasi.

Even though Govind wanted to go for the civil services through school, IAS always seemed beyond reach, mostly because of poverty. The condition of the family became even worse when his father got a serious leg injury and could no long pull rickshaw. Govind still managed to find room for his dream and became an IAS officer at an age of 23.

❖ K. Jayaganesh – From Waiter to an IAS Officer

If you don't believe in the mantra of trying again and again regardless of how many times you've already failed, may be you ought to go through K. Jayaganesh's journey of becoming an IAS officer. The man hails from a poor family in Tamil Nadu and did many odd jobs, including working as a waiter, before make his dream come true.

Setting an example for IAS aspirants, Jayaganesh secured 156th rank the seventh time (his last chance) and got selected for Indian Administrative Services after failing the civil services exam for six times! Krishnan, Jayaganesh's father worked as a supervisor in a factory, brought him up in Vinavamangalam, a small village in Vellore district. Jayaganesh is the eldest of his siblings (a brother and two sisters) and completed his schooling after studying in the village up to the 8th standard.

❖ Gopala Sundara Raj and R.V. Karnan – The Rank-holders who dodged all the Hurdles

In the year 2012, Gopala Sundara Raj and R.V. Karnan secured the 5th and the 158th ranks respectively in the Civil Services Exam results. Raj comes from Ramanathapuram district of Tamil Nadu and R.V. Karnan hails from Karaikudi city of Sivaganga district of the same state.

Raj's parents, who couldn't study beyond primary school in their childhood, always wanted to put him in English medium background of school but had to drop the idea just because of bad financial conditions. However, they could not believe it when their son cleared IAS despite not having studied in a sophisticated environment, proving that poverty can never be an obstruction in the way of success if you are dedicated to your dreams.

❖ Rashmi Zagade – The Only Lady IAS Officer from Pune in 2010

Rashmi Siddharth Zagade from Pune began her IAS saga in 2003 and clicked it in 2010 to become the only lady IAS officer from the whole of Pune City in the same year. Inspiringly, after making four unsuccessful attempts before, the 29 year old finally bagged 169th rank among more than 800 candidates and proudly gave the credit to Siddharth Zagade, her school drop-out husband.

Despite seeing a great deal of failure previous to her success, that is, four consecutive failed attempts, Rashmi did not give up, and went on with determination and support from her husband. And after making it to the interview stage the fourth time, she took a year's break to prepare further and never looked back. Rashmi dropped geography and opted for history before reappearing this time when she ultimately did it. Why she credited her husband for her success was because it was he who prodded her to appear for IAS, even when, being a science graduate, she had no idea what this exam was all about.

Conclusion

When you're motivated, you have a desire to become an IAS. Motivation pushes you towards your goal because of a desire for IAS. Motivation helps you clarify your goal, so you know exactly what you're working towards.

Once you know what your goal is, motivation helps you prioritise your life. If your goal is to become IAS, you need to set time aside each day to achieve it. Motivation helps you to focus and make a commitment to seeing your goal accomplished.

Every road to success will have a setback. There is no such thing as a dream route to reach your dreams. Setbacks will have you doubt whether your goal is worth the effort, but motivation steps in and gives you the strength and courage to try again.

Benjamin Franklin says, by failing to prepare today, you will be preparing to fail tomorrow. Be prepared now. Prepare today and tomorrow will be an easy sail.

I know that it is not as easy as it appears. One goes through hell lot of difficulties during the exam preparation.

Winston Churchill—"If you are going through hell, keep going."

If today is lived as it should be, tomorrow shall be a good day. Just keep going.

❑❑❑

4

How to have a Focused Mind?

Introduction

"Focus On Where You Want To Go Not On What You Fear."– Anthony Robbins.

Being able to focus is a skill; a skill that most of us take for granted. We must all learn to focus on the really important tasks that will have the greatest impact on achieving our happiness and goals in life. We just cannot afford to spend valuable time to aimlessly go through life doing the easy stuff that anybody can do.

In order to accomplish meaningful goals we must focus like a laser beam on what really matters at our jobs and in our private lives. Our brain thinks more than one thought at a time. Thus, we must think about, focus on, and complete only the tasks that are most important to us right now.

Importance of Focus for an IAS Aspirant

Focus is the one word that has to be on the top of any IAS aspirant's preparation checklist. It is one of 'the' most important qualities of a serious aspirant. It is a major factor in your success in this examination. Every other aspirant is serious, but not many are pin-point focused. This is what makes much of the difference.

UPSC IAS Examination is not an easy exam to crack. It needs well-devised strategy, hard work, and dedication. Improving your focus can make you achieve the dream of becoming a good and an efficient IAS officer. You should have a dream in your life. Mold a dream and work hard for achieving that dream.

If you want to enhance your focus, then you need to learn to avoid disturbances. UPSC IAS Exam is not about testing knowledge; it is all about testing a person's maturity, action, thought process, decision-making skill and a lot many more.

Here we are giving some tips to focus on your aim and to crack UPSC IAS Exam. These small tips can bring a big change in your life.

❖ F – Follow; O – Organize; C – Craft; U – Unambiguous; S – Self Assessment

- **Follow your Goal:** Without a right strategy, aspirant cannot achieve the goal of becoming an IAS officer. Once the aspirants start preparing for Civil Services IAS Examination, they should make a well-devised strategy and study plan. The syllabus of UPSC IAS Exam is diverse and vast. That does not mean one should know everything under the sun.
- **Organize:** UPSC aspirants should be organized. There are many benefits being organized. The aspirants will be able to be more focused on what they want to achieve. This will help UPSC aspirants to set and achieve their goals in a more efficient manner. The energy and enthusiasm gained from good lifestyle habits are necessary to motivate you at every step of life.
- **Craft a study plan:** Having a goal in your life makes you stay more focused. Towards achieving your goal and stayed focus to become an IAS is not an easy task. But you have a clearly defined goal, you can achieve the dream. UPSC IAS exam is the hardest exam in the country. Break this big goal into small goals. Here aspirants can break down syllabus into small parts. Setting appropriate and achievable goals will help you to complete the vast syllabus. Setting these types of goals will help you to crack UPSC Exam.
- **Unambiguous Time Management:** Time and tide wait for none. Time management is an important aspect of UPSC IAS Exam. Make an unambiguous time management and stick to it. From the preparation time to the examination hall, one should effectively use and handle the time.
- **Self-assessment:** Self-assessment is important to stay focused on your goals. In the journey towards Mussoorie, you should know your efficiency and capability and self-assessment will help you to stay focused.

- **Know when to say no:** Some aspirants often put their goals aside for emotions, people or other things. Aspirants should say no to those things which would deviate from their goals. They should say no strictly towards the negative energy which tries to override them. A well organized and articulated person only knows about how to ward off such distractions.
- **Physical exercises:** Any sort of daily physical exercise, like running or yoga, helps you to dwell in the present as your mind's awareness remains on your breath and body. Some form of physical activity also helps in developing mental strength and willpower. Increased mental strength will enable you to bring back your focus on your goal when you astray.

❖ Distractions in Thoughts

- **It happens to all of us:** You're working away on something you've got to get done, and suddenly you realize that for quite some time you've been lost in a reverie about something else entirely. You don't know when your mind went off track, nor how long you've been meandering down this one.
- **Our minds wander on average 50 percent of the time:** The exact rate varies enormously. When Harvard researchers had 2,250 people report what they were doing and what they were thinking about at random points throughout their day, the doing-thinking gaps ranged widely.
- **The biggest gap was during work:** Mind-wandering is epidemic on the job. Try these simple suggestions for slowing things down.

Here are some suggestions which will help in improving your concentration and memory, you will gain greater perspective on your life, and you'll be able to think more clearly and with less effort.

Witness your Thoughts

No one can stop thinking entirely; it is impossible. If you start trying not to think, you only end up thinking about how to stop thinking! What you can do, however, is to withdraw from your thoughts and become more of an objective spectator.

❖ Picture your Mind as a Blank Canvas or a Dark Sky

Allow your thoughts to come and go, but resist the urge to follow each one. Your brain will eventually slow down and you will feel less pressured.

❖ Count Thoughts

If you find it difficult to let go of your thoughts, try counting slowly as you breathe. Watch your thoughts and try to resist following them. Turn your attention to the count as you breathe out.

❖ Pay Active Attention

As you work and think, try to keep your attention on the task at hand. Be strict with yourself and each time your mind wanders, return it to the task. As you keep refocusing your attention, your "mind stillness" will improve.

❖ Still your Body

One sign of fragmented attention is fragmented movement. For example, when you are at the theatre, it is easy to tell if others around you are fully attentive to the performance. People who sniff and sigh, move their heads this way and that, and wiggle in their seats are having some difficulty in concentrating. Rapt attention is usually accompanied by still body posture.

❖ Find a comfortable position and don't allow yourself to move

Concentrate on what you are doing or watching, drawing your attention away from physical distractions, and focus your thoughts on your task. After a while, you will notice that you fidget less and feel less physical discomfort. You are now channeled into mental exertion.

❖ Interest your Mind

Try to find interest in projects to help you concentrate. Taking up a new hobby can be a tremendous help. You should also try to find something interesting even in the dullest chore. If you are at a gathering, find someone and start a conversation. Be inquisitive and you might discover you have similar interests.

❖ Open the Mind

Just as strength, stamina and flexibility must be incorporated in your physical routine, the mind needs new and absorbing challenges to give it a change from its everyday journey. Notice something new on the same way home that you might not have noticed before. Buy a magazine on a subject you normally wouldn't look at, read it, and open yourself to new possibilities.

❖ Manage your Temptations

Many of the distractors that pull us away from what we're working on are digital: tweets, emails, and the like. There are several apps that can wall off those temptations to wander off. Chrome has two free apps that do this: Nanny for Google blocks off websites you might be tempted to visit, for whatever length of time you decide; StayFocusd limits the amount of time (also set by you) you can spend in your inbox, on Facebook, or wherever else you might be seduced away.

❖ Monitor your Mind and take Second Thoughts

Noticing where your mind has gone – checking your twitter feed instead of working on that report – gives you the chance for a second thought: "my mind has wandered off again." That very thought disengages your brain from where it has wandered and activates brain circuits that can help your attention get unstuck and return to the work at hand.

❖ Practice a Daily Mindfulness Session

This mental exercise can be as simple as watching your breath, noticing when your mind has wandered off, letting go of the wandering thought and bringing it back to your breath again. These movements of the mind are like a mental workout, the equivalent of repetitions in lifting free weights: every rep strengthens the muscle a bit more. In mindfulness what gets stronger are the brain's circuits for noticing when your mind has wandered, letting go, and returning to your chosen focus. And that's just what we need to stay with during that one important task we're working on.

Some Daily Activities to Increase Your Focus

❖ Start Small

You only need to focus for one minute at first. Clear everything away, pick your one important task, and just do it for one minute without switching. This is hard to do in the beginning but if you consciously focus on focusing, you can do it. It's just a minute.

❖ Reward Yourself

The reward for focusing for one minute can be one minute (or 30 seconds) of checking whatever you want. Email, Facebook, whatever. Or get up and take a one-minute walk. Stretch, drink some water, massage your neck, enjoy your small victory. Empires are created with small victories.

❖ Repeat

Keep doing one minute focus, one minute reward (or 1 minute to 30 seconds if you like) for about half an hour (15 of each). You're done. Repeat that later in the day. Rejoice in how much work you got done! And notice how you've set up a positive feedback cycle for focusing.

❖ Increase in Small Steps

Tomorrow, make it two minutes on, one minute off. Repeat that for 30 minutes, do it later in the day too. Feel free to go wild and do three focus sessions in a day if you like, but it's not necessary.

❖ Keep taking Baby Steps

I think you can see the pattern by now. Make it three minutes on, one minute off on the third day, then 4:1, then 5:1. When you get to 10 minutes, be crazy and take a 2 minute break. When you get to

20 minutes, take a 3 minute break. At 30 minutes of focus, you've earned a 5 minute break. And once you're at 30 minutes, you can stay there. No need to become a monk.

Conclusion

As UPSC preparation is very different from the kind of study done in schools or colleges. Most of the aspirants fall short in producing this quality in the preparation stage. A major chunk of them have always been the habit of last minute studying. Thus, focus is seen only one day before the exam! But, for this examination, 'focus everyday' is a much needed skill that needs to be developed. Only when the mind is completely immersed in the topic that you are reading, you can be most productive.

Developing focus is more like developing a skill. This means that with practice it can be developed. Scientific research about the mind says, "Our mind perfects what it practices the most, be it good or bad". With the advent of android-smart phone technology, plethora of social-networking sites and ten million other things to distract one from his goal, our mind is in the constant practice of wandering and jumping from present to past or future. And an exam like such can lead one's mind inevitably into the future uncertainties and risks. Hence, to practice being in the present, taking one day at a time and being 'focused' are the exams that one has to pass along with the actual examination.

❑❑❑

5

Why DAF Preparation is Important for a Personality Test?

Introduction

The UPSC gave an interview call to nearly 2,500 candidates. It organises every day several boards, each headed by a UPSC member and comprising four to five other members, usually experts from different fields. The board conducts the interview by posing questions, seeking views and assessing the objective appreciation of a candidate regarding different issues of national and international significance. It also tests the candidates in areas related to their personal profile as disclosed in their 'Detailed Application Form' (DAF) submitted to the UPSC.

Personality Test

To give a full and clear insight of the Personality Test (Interview), UPSC explains and clarifies in detail:

"The candidate will be interviewed by a Board who will have before them a record of his/her career. He/she will be asked questions on matters of general interest. The object of the interview is to assess the personal suitability of the candidate for a career in public service by a Board of competent and unbiased observers. The test is intended to judge the mental caliber of a candidate. In broad terms this is really an assessment of not only his/her intellectual qualities but also social traits and his/her interest in current affairs. Some of the qualities to be judged are mental alertness, critical powers of assimilation, clear and logical exposition, balance of judgement, variety and depth of interest, ability for social cohesion and leadership, intellectual and moral integrity".

"The technique of the interview is not that of a strict cross-examination but of a natural, though directed and purposive conversation which is intended to reveal the mental qualities of the candidate."

"The interview test is not intended to be a test either of the specialised or general knowledge of the candidates which has been already tested through their written papers. Candidates are expected to have taken an intelligent interest not only in their special subjects of academic study but also in the events which are happening around them both within and outside their own state or country as well as in modern currents of thought and in new discoveries which should rouse the curiosity of well educated youth."

Why DAF is Important?

From reading above thing, it is clear that, it is a test of personality which is reflected in your DAF like hobbies, your background, your expression of opinions without hesitation etc. DAF stands for Detailed Application Form, is a very crucial document and it defines everything from the career of a candidate to their posting. Prepare each and every word of this thoroughly. Interview marks decide your rank and more than half of the interview is based on your DAF.

Mindset of the Interviewer

Mostly UPSC interviewer are accomplished Bureaucrats, Academicians or people from Armed Forces (in age 40's, 50's and 60's). They are highly experienced and have mostly met thousands of people like you and me.

They expect clarity, confidence, integrity, humility, administrator like qualities and conviction from an aspirant which is clearly reflected in your DAF and way of your expression at the time of interview.

Interviewee

You are accountable to each and every word you are putting in DAF. So, fill everything taking into consideration that any question can be asked from whatever you are writing. Be ready for next 4, 5 questions from every word you are putting. Sometimes (though rarely), from a single hobby/extra-curricular activity/area of interest your interview may start and whole interview may go in particular direction. The single word may determine your future.

Actually, after the mains result you have very little time to prepare and if you have filled DAF in very casual way then it impacts your confidence at that time. However, if you have filled it with care then you will know the areas you are comfortable and if provided chance you can direct the whole interview in the direction you are comfortable. (obviously, it depends on your smartness at time of interview).

Analysis of DAF

❖ Date of birth and age

Remember any special occasions related with your birth date, month or year like birth of any freedom fighter, great scientists or any unique festival celebrated in that month or year. For example, if you are born on Gandhi Jayanti, it is obvious that you should prepare about Gandhi, his role in freedom movement, his values embedded in constitution, his message to the nation etc.

❖ Address

Remember Special features, peculiarities, typical problems, famous persons and places etc., related to your address. Also remember any important historical events associated with any of them, upcoming events in your city, its history, culture and heritage, the running schemes, what can be done better, what needs updation, best practices observed if any. Stay relevant and try to have a critical perspective when preparing such points.

❖ Gender

Prepare some gender sensitive issues like gender inequality in politics, economy, education, nutrition, health, feminism concepts, some gender relative schemes of state and central government etc.

❖ Marital Status

If you are married, prepare on importance of marriage in Indian society, its role in society, globalization, impact on working couples and recent current affairs like infidelity laws etc.

❖ Citizenship and Nationality

Prepare well on nationality related issues, citizenship articles in constitution, refugee problems related to citizenship, some opinions on what is nationalism in a balanced way.

❖ Mother Tongue

There can be chance that some board members may know your mother tongue or may be they are of same language so gain some knowledge on history of your mother tongue, literature related to it and some famous personalities in literature in that language, present status of your language like is it a classical language or eighth schedule language or endangered language.

❖ Place of Birth

Learn some features, famous festivals, any specialities associated to your birth place, meaning and importance of that place if any, population, sex ratio etc., in that area or state.

❖ Community

Candidates belonging to other backward classes, scheduled classes and minorities etc., should prepare articles and provisions related to them in constitution, schemes and policies related to them, status of their communities, balanced opinions on reservations and on recent agitations by some other communities for reservation. Note you should not be very critical about those issues.

❖ Disabled People

Persons with disabilities should prepare on recent initiatives by the governments related to disabilities, the recent legislation on disabilities and how it empowers them. They should also develop some innovative ideas to improve their position in the society.

❖ Choice of Centre of Examination

Know about the city from where you wrote your prelims and mains, their history, uniqueness, food, culture, issues and suggestions for improvement. And also be prepared for the questions, for example, why did you give your exam from Delhi if you belong to Chennai, why you have given your prelims and mains from two different cities etc., if you are from a different state and you are giving exam in Delhi or Hyderabad be prepared for this question as you and UPSC already knows that these two cities are coaching hubs of UPSC.

❖ Indian Language Paper and Optional Subject

This is very important area of questions. Need to prepare this well. Revise basics, be up-to-date with recent developments. Use google alerts to stay updated on any recent development on particular topics. If your subject of graduation is not your optional, it is advisable to prepare an answer to the reason why. Also you need to brush up the basics of your graduation subject.

Questions on optionals are usually fact based. If you know the answer, it's great. However if you don't, do not panic. They are asked only to test your resilience and ability to respond to pressure. You can have no answer to twenty of these questions in a row and still get 200+ marks. What you can't get away with is not answering an opinion based question on the 21st instance. So, be calm and handle such questions with confidence.

❖ Language Medium for Mains and Interview

Not a fluent grip but you should have a basic skill of understanding, listening, reading and writing in the language you have opted, if you opt for regional languages then prepare some basic questions on that language.

❖ Names of Parents, their Profession, Income, Address of your Parents

Know the meaning of your parents name, details about their profession for example, if your parents are handicrafts makers, learn about different types of handicrafts etc., details related to the address like special geographical features, political issues in that state, administrative issues in the state for instance learn about red corridor and Naxalism and security issues if your state is in red corridor, or learn about backward regions grant fund if your district is in backward region etc., because UPSC always favours a person who has some knowledge about their background and state.

❖ Educational Qualifications

Prepare well on your graduation and post-graduation subjects and new developments in those subjects, for example, if you are from electronics background, be ready for questions like artificial intelligence, electric mobility, robotics etc., know the meanings of names, historical importance or any peculiarities of your schools, colleges and university, for instance, if you study in a college named, Gurunanak College, it is better to know about that name and history associated with that name.

❖ Employment

Prepare for questions on your previous professions/jobs and organisation, if any. Reasons for a long time gap after graduation without employment, if any. Prepare for questions if you have worked in any foreign countries for example, geography of that country, importance of that country to India, Brain Drain etc.

❖ Hobbies, Awards and any Extra-Curricular Activities

Hobbies form another important question area—Be honest. Do not cook up. So whatever you have mentioned as your hobby, try to gain expertise in it (both theoretical and practical) in these few weeks.

For example, Arpita Shukla had mentioned reading fiction as her hobby. She was asked the name of her favourite book, favourite author, the Man Booker winners, why Indian authors don't feature big on the international scene etc., because if you fill something you should have practical knowledge of it, it shows your integrity.

❖ Home State

This is very important area and you should have a good knowledge about your home state like its geography, economy, culture, social issues in your state, political affairs of state etc., for example, in 2015 a candidate from Telangana was asked about the outstanding issues after the bifurcation of state and from thereon he was asked 8 questions on the home state topic out of 14 questions and he scored 198 marks in interview.

Cadre Allocation and Service Preference

Questions on preferences in services or cadres are not being asked too frequently nowadays. However, you should prepare a reasonable, brief answer for your order of preferences in both the services as well as the cadre. Discuss it with friends, family and seniors and come up with a personal and honest reply, justification for the same, especially when it is unusual. e.g. why IPS and not IAS or IFS?

Revised Order of Preferences for Services: justification for the same

The tenor of the interview is that of a purposeful conversation. The objective is the assessment of the thoughts and overall personality of the candidate and not merely bookish knowledge or even theoretical concepts, with the latter already being an area of evaluation in the main examination.

What the board usually endeavours to assess in the aspirants, is her/his sincerity of purpose, clarity of thoughts and expression, balance of judgement, ability to reason, to think critically, analytically in a wholistic way, positiveness of approach, awareness and concern for socio-economic issues and problems, inter alia other attributes. But what is of utmost importance is the ability to think with an honest approach, sincerity of purpose and willingness to toil hard.

Remember it's your personality test, the more you are truthful, the more your DAF shows that you are committed and dedicated to whatever you have written (a sign of integrity) the more marks you will fetch! ❑❑❑

6

Importance of Being a Civil Servant after a Good Performance in Interview

Introduction

The candidates getting qualifying marks in the written examination are called for interview. The aim of interview is to test the personality of the candidates and therefore, it is referred to as the personality test. The UPSC takes a decision on qualifying marks. What will be the number of candidates to be called for interview or Personality test is dependent on the number of vacancies. This test is also important for the recruitment. The examiners test strength to be an administrator, presence of mind, the ability to run the administration, the mental strength to fall any situation. The candidate must have courage of mind. India is a multicultural state with some main languages and a large number of dialects. Above all, there are numerous religious groups. In the midst of all these the IAS officer will have to run the administration.

Preparing a Civil Servant

The candidates who clear the personality test are announced by the UPSC fit for the job and they are thus recruited. However, the recruitment does not mean joining the services. All the successful candidates will have to undergo stringent training and thus, the training is the most important part of recruitment. There are three types of training. The first one is Foundational Training. The candidates selected are sent to National Academy of Administration. It is located at Mussoorie. This Academy has been named after our former Prime Minister Lal Bahadur Shastri. This foundational training is very important. The candidates who are selected come from different academic institutions, social, economic and cultural backgrounds and therefore, obviously they need common training and certain common instructions. In order to be a good administrator a person must have a clear and deep knowledge about social, economic, cultural and other aspects of India. He must have a preliminary idea about India's culture and civilization. The purpose of foundational training is to impart an idea on these subjects. The foundational course enables a candidate to be acquainted with important aspects of Republic of India. Persons from different backgrounds have given significance to this foundational training. Another aspect or part of the foundational training is the persons who are told to visit different parts, especially of rural areas of India and they are told to prepare report on their observations. This is significant because the reports highlight the mental ability and observational power. The foundational training also includes physical training, games, exercise, swimming, horse riding along with training of yoga. At the end of foundational training, the candidates are told to participate in a written examination and marks are awarded to candidates and these are added to the marks that they obtained in the UPSC examination. Once the foundational training is completed, the candidates make a visit to their respective training centres. This means, the candidates, selected for IPS, go to the National Police Academy, Hyderabad. Here the candidates of IPS category receive training on police service. But the trainees of IAS continue to study at National Academy of Administration.

This follows the professional training, which is a sandwich programming between two phases. The first phase, whose duration is three months, usually covers topics of concern to the IAS like law and order, land revenue etc. The training methodology comprises of lecture, discussions, syndicate work, debates etc. By the end of the first phase of training, there is a written examination whose marks are taken into consideration while calculating the final ranking in the service. Then the district training starts under the supervision of a carefully selected district collector in the state to which an officer is allotted. This is on-the-job training, the trainee getting a feel of administration and obtaining an experience of different field level positions in the district. It is believed that this is a very crucial stage of professional training and even an important stage of training. During the period of professional training, a trainee is made to visit a district to enrich practical experience. Today all across India, panchayati raj system has come into effect and panchayat is taking part in all types of state administration. Particularly, the panchayati raj is a part of all works related to development. For this reason, district level training is very significant.

Many are of the belief that (and it is true) the success (even it may be brilliant) in the written examination cannot make a man a good administrator. He must undergo a number of serious and rigorous training. In the absence of proper training, a person can never become a good administrator. In all countries, enough emphasis is given to the proper training. A candidate can be successful in the written examination, but a good scholar cannot always be a good administrator. Administration means governance and for good governance, a person must be given proper training. Again, training is a continuous process. New situation arises, problems crop up, and the administrator must be prepared to meet the situation and solve the problem. Because of the immense importance of training both IAS and IPS, the trainees are sent to districts and in remote areas. The simple purpose is that candidates must be ready to face the realities. This practical experience will help them to be a good administrator. Talking of practical experience, we come to know that the significance of IAS and IPS officers is increasing—specifically in parliamentary form of government. In this form of government, both legislature and executive undergo change after certain period of time. Obviously, the whole burden of state administration falls upon the bureaucrats or civil servants. This indirectly means that the civil servants, in parliamentary system, are the key figures of state administration. Therefore, the situation that arises out of the above discussion is that the bureaucrats must be good administrators and that largely depends on the type of training they receive. Every bureaucrat must have proper training and experience about different aspects of society. So, only through training, a man becomes a good administrator.

Training is a vital component of civil service and all required emphasis is given to this. The Government of India has constructed two reputed institutions for proper training — one for IAS officers and the other for IPS officers. A large amount of money is spent for training and maintenance of these institutes. But many people have raised doubts about the efficacy of the long and costly process and programmes of training. To the officer undergoing training, 'training is a stimulant'. They try to use the period of training by doing the work they have been asked to do. They gather practical experience and during their service, they utilize it. It has been maintained that training stimulates them in different ways, such as to do something for the people, to gather experience, and they apply the experience when they start to work as an administrator. When many trainees meet together, they exchange views among them. In the era of globalization and liberalization, there is a great significance of bureaucracy and the training. It is usually seen that the world today (in the age of liberalization) has become a big village or a single unit. The states, big or small, are influenced by each other and this influence falls upon the public administration. If the public administration is not well equipped, it is not properly trained, it will not be able to adjust itself with the changes that are taking place. Particularly the public administration of a developing nation like India must be capable of adjusting itself with the changes that are regularly taking place everywhere. Because of this experts are talking about proper training for civil servants. The idea of good governance also appears. An efficient and able public administration is capable of meeting any situation and can assure good governance. In an age of globalization a well-equipped and well trained public administration can meet any situation and can help the speed of development to the vital key to progress lies in both selection of public servants and their proper training.

Comprehending Civil Service

The Civil Services denote the permanent executive branch of the Republic of India which is the regarded as the backbone of the administrative machinery of the country. In the parliamentary democracy of India, the ultimate responsibility to run the administration rests with the elected representatives of the people, who are the ministers. But a handful of ministers cannot be expected to deal personally with multiple problems of modern administration. Thus, the ministers design the policy and it is for the civil servants to execute this policy. The Indian civil servants implement the decisions of executive. The members of civil service serve at the pleasure of the President of India and Article 311 of the constitution protects them from politically motivated or vindictive action. Civil servants are employees of the Government of India or of the states; however, not all employees of the Government are civil servants. Civil servants in an individual capacity are paid as per the Civil List. Senior civil servants may be called to account by Parliament. The members of the civil services represent as administrators in the central government and state government; emissaries in the foreign missions/embassies; as tax collectors and revenue commissioners; as civil service commissioned police officers; as permanent representative(s) and employees in the United Nations and its agencies and as Chairman, Managing Director, full-time functional Director/Member of the Board of Management of various Public Sector Undertakings/Enterprises, Corporations, Banks and financial institutions. Civil servants are employed to different agencies of India and can also be chosen as advisors or special duty officers or private secretaries to ministers of the Union and the State Government. The highest-ranking civil servant is appointed as the Cabinet Secretary. He is ex-officio Chairman of the Civil Services Board; the chief of the Indian Administrative Service and head of all civil services under the rules of business of the Government of India. He also holds the 11th position in the Order of Precedence of India. The position holder is accountable to ensure that the Civil Service is equipped with the skills and abilities to meet the everyday challenges it faces and that civil servants work in a fair and decent environment.

Comprehending IAS/IPS Positions

The Indian Administrative Service, usually abbreviated as IAS, is regarded as one of the two premier civil services of India.

IAS officers are appointed in strategic and key positions in the Union Government, States governments and public-sector undertakings. As in other countries following the Westminster system of government, IAS as the permanent bureaucracy in India is an inseparable part of the executive of the Government of India, and therefore, provides neutrality and continuity to the administration. On conforming to service after probation as Sub-Divisional Magistrate, an IAS officer is given the administrative command in the district as District Magistrate and Collector after a few years of service, and normally after sixteen years of service in some states, an IAS officer heads a whole division in the state, as its Commissioner. On attaining the Apex Scale, IAS officers go on to head whole Departments and Ministries of the Government of India. IAS officers represent the Government of India at the international level in bilateral and multilateral negotiations. On deputations, they work at Intergovernmental organizations like World Bank, International Monetary Fund, Asian Development Bank and United Nations or its Agencies. IAS officers at different levels of administration play an important role in conducting free, fair and smooth elections in India under the guidance of Election Commission of India.

Conclusion

The civil services in India are an important stakeholder in governing rules and implementing policies. It has an important role in the Indian governance system. From the British rule in India, civil services has been undergoing transformation and over time, the system has been made more effective in its operations as the role of civil services has seen a lot of changes. Presently, fast economic growth has resulted in an increase in the quantum of work. The Government is not perceived as a law enforcer or a controller of national resources. It is progressively viewed as an efficient provider of basic services and public goods. Populace of India expect from Government to facilitate growth and development. With reference to civil services, civil servants have been trained to deal with upcoming challenges arising out of globalization. They will have to shift their orientation from being controllers to facilitators and from being providers to enablers. They need to prepare themselves with the essential skills and capabilities to tackle these new challenges. For the growth of nation, they would require to have proficiency in new technologies and new styles of functioning.

❑❑❑

7

All About UPSC IAS Interviews

The UPSC is a central agency of India that is authorized to conduct the Civil Services Examination, Indian Forest Service examination, Engineering Services Examination, Combined Defence Services Examination, National Defence Academy Examination, Naval Academy Examination, Combined Medical Services Examination, Special Class Railway Apprentice, Indian Economic Service/Indian Statistical Service Examination, Combined Geoscientist and Geologist Examination, as well as Central Armed Police Forces (Assistant Commandant) examination.

The last step of an IAS Exam is the Interview. But, it is crucial as well because every single mark at this stage can decide your fate. A bad day of interview can spoil the chances of a good career. Before interviews, some students have high enough marks in the merit list while others just make the cutoff. It is very tough for the marginal candidates to get a post without an extraordinary performance during interview. So, every candidate who goes out at interview should prepare in such a way that even if he is at the margins, he could be there in the final list, else all his efforts will be of no use.

Interview for Government Exam

It is to be noted that unlike written tests, interview marks depend more on the impression of the candidate on the interviewer, the candidate's conduct and behavioural traits. UPSC does not check the raw knowledge of the candidate, it checks their personality.

Some tips to follow to do well in interview are the following:

1. ***Knowing Yourself Well is Important:*** It is very crucial to be wholly aware about yourself, your strengths and your weaknesses. It begins with filling in the interview form which comprises of your past experiences and your personal details. The first question that you are going to encounter in the

Interview hall is, 'Tell us something about yourself' or 'Please introduce yourself'. This is a simple question with a constant answer. But still many students fail to make the most of this question either because they undermine the importance of introduction or are not confident about themselves. If you are about to answer this question in a smooth manner you will gain in two ways. One, the panel members will feel comfortable about you. Second, you will feel relaxed because the first impression is very important. They also ask a lot of questions from your bio-data, therefore it is very important to be true and comfortable while answering questions about your personal experiences and interests. Besides knowing yourself, you should also be well acquainted with the State and District you belong to. Your community or religion can also lead to a stream of questions. Knowing yourself well not only gives you the confidence and ease of answering questions about you, it also gives you a potent weapon i.e. to give a direction to the interview. In case you are well aware about what you know best, you can write about it in the bio-data. They will surely ask questions from bio-data. Similarly, avoid writing or speaking about the topics about your difficult areas. For instance, in case you don't want to mention about some of the places you have lived in, you don't have to in your introduction or bio-data.

2. ***Logic and Consistency of Thought:*** Talking of their thought process, interviewers expect the candidates to be confident. You should have well developed rationale so that you can present your argument in a confident way even when the interviews try to oppose your point of view. This doesn't mean that you have to prove yourself right on every point. You have to support your arguments and viewpoints with valid statements. Your statements need to be consistent with each other. You also need to make sure that you are totally calm when your arguments are refuted by the members. You can logically think well only when you listen to them carefully and grasp their point of view.

3. ***Scope and Depth of Understanding:*** The interview also tests the scope and depth of candidate's understanding of the world. While the candidates can get away in written exams with reproducing concepts read in books, the interview gives the tool to see how much of that knowledge is imbibed by the candidate. This is because the candidate gets very little time to think before the answering. Whatever a candidate utters gives an idea about how well and minutely he comprehends the events taking place in and around him.
4. ***Care for the Society:*** As you are appearing for the Civil Services, you have to show that you have a strong feeling for the society. They will ask many questions which will require your viewpoint on the prevailing social issues. They want to see if you want to get into the civil services for personal gains or for the sake of society. It is not possible that everyone is motivated to serve the society. So, you have to put yourself in the shoes of a patriot and respond accordingly. If you have a natural inclination for society, it is very good else you will have to inculcate a love for the society as it is very tough to fool them with fake sympathy for the society.
5. ***Skill to Communicate:*** It is to be noted that whatever you try to say reaches the panel members in a vivid and crisp manner. You should make use of your words very carefully. Never think that the members of the panel are very learned and will understand technical language. Each of them is from different background. If you are asked a science question, don't reply in the manner that only he can understand your answer. Your reply should address and satisfy all the panel members. This is because your final rating will be done by adding the individual ratings of different members sitting in the room.
6. ***Selecting Reliable Sources:*** It is worth-noting to understand what a dependable source of information is and what is not. Media News channels like Aaj Tak or Times Now, etc. are not dependable source of information. On the other hand, DD News is a reliable source. Similar is the case with print media and books. Use of unreliable sources of information can

affect your impression as well as answers. Therefore, you should keep yourself away from these sources. Bad sources for UPSC interviewers are something similar to prohibited substances for sportsmen.

7. ***A Pleasant Nature:*** Probably, interviewers are going to make it easy for you if you are pleasant and cheerful with them. You may be a bit nervous at times but you should come up with occasional smile. This will help ease the tensions in the atmosphere and also give you some time to think out the answers. This also tells about your social traits. A good leader is expected to have a control over different situations and should make the situation comfortable for all.

What Is Not Expected during the Interviews

Many myths are associated with the objectives of the Personal Interviews which need to be kept out of mind before going to the interview. Some of these are mentioned below:

1. ***Flawless Vocabulary:*** Good communication doesn't mean that you should have a flashy vocabulary or a fast accent. In reality, it is advised that you should abstain from using uncommon words. This is due to the fact that you are more likely to use a wrong word by using difficult words. Even if you can't think of the best word try to complete the sentence with basic words. This will let the panel know that you don't have an English speaking background and they will adjust to you. Also, try to avoid commenting on their statements with phrases like 'I agree', 'of course', etc. Make all efforts to behave like a student who behaves in front of a teacher.

2. ***General Knowledge Based on Facts:*** Among the candidates, the most common fear while going to an interview is the failure to answer questions. It should be made clear that your achievement in the interview is not assessed by the number or the percentage of correct answers. Besides this, knowledge of the subjects has already been tested via extensive mains tests. There is no need for the panel to test you again on the same criteria.

3. ***Final Answers:*** While putting forth your view point or analysis on a subject, make an attempt to use the phrases such as 'I think' and 'According to me'. This will enable them to be more cordial with you and they may themselves come up with the right answers in case you are not right. On the other hand, if you try to draw conclusions as if you can't be wrong, they may get irritated and may land you in tricky questions. It is a delicate area and you have to appease them to your side. On the whole, good interviews are those which are mostly in the form of casual interactions.

❑❑❑

8

Important Tips for Cracking IAS/IPS Interview

IAS Interview is considered as the last phase of selection criterion for IAS exam. Interview is conducted to assess the character of the applicant. The committee which conducts interview comprises one head and members who are specialists in their specific fields. Questions are put up randomly from any field, be it academic or non-academic. The committee members of IAS interview board attempt to assess the full personality of a candidate in a few minutes. Many applicants are scared of facing IAS Interview board as they turn out to be nervous, but if you have cleared IAS Mains, then you certainly are very intelligent and can definitely clear IAS Interview. You must have confidence and trust in you.

To feel at ease in decoding the character of an IAS or IPS interview, we have the following tips that you can embrace while you initiate preparing for the same:

- ***Initiate your Preparation for Interview from January Onwards:*** The most important step is to start early while preparing for the interview stage. If you start preparing from the start of the year, you will automatically get at least 3 months to prepare yourself for the finale. I also suggest you to start preparing from one year in advance so that you get enough time.
- ***Respect members who will take your Interview:*** After entering the interview room, pay due respect to the members who will take your interview. The committee will observe your mannerism and decide whether you will be fit or not. So take mannerism seriously.
- ***Remember what you wrote in your Mains Exam:*** One can appear for the interview only after he/she successfully clears the written mains exam. Therefore, while you give interview, you

may be asked what you did in your mains. So remember and revise what you wrote there.

- ***Have Positive Views in Your Mind:*** Having a positive mindset is must while going for an interview. Usually, it happens that negative thoughts would start coming to your mind. Specially, who are giving interview for the first time. So be positive and think right.
- ***Have proper command on Your Language Skills:*** Your medium of the interview (English or Hindi) does not matter much. What matters is the command over the particular language.
- ***It takes more courage to listen than to speak:*** Listening is more important to respond properly. So, it is best to listen completely and then answer rather interrupting when they are speaking.
- ***First question: why you want to join IAS?*** Prepare for the most usual question, that is, why you want to join IAS. This will be perhaps the first question that you have to answer. So prepare an honest reply beforehand. You will find it easy to answer.
- ***Speak Your Heart and do not lie to yourself:*** If you face a situation where you find questions to be tough, then do not tell a lie. Never create a fake story to boost yourself. Just tell them truthfully, it does not really matters.
- ***Show Confidence and talk to them, not at them:*** Making eye contact is a must for effective communication. You should always look into their eyes and then talk. This is very basic interview tip for a civil service interview. Lack of eye contact lets them think that you do not have self-confidence.
- ***For Serious Question give a Serious Reply:*** Although you should give a smile and give answers laughingly, if you confront a serious question, then your answer should be serious too. You have to display them that you care about what they are asking.
- ***Prepare what you will to Say for Hobby Section:*** The question about your hobby is a very serious and common question in a civil service interview. You should answer this question in a

light mood. The board members must get a chance to laugh at some point in time.

Predictable Interview Questions

The Kothari Committee of the UPSC enumerated the abilities that should be rated in the interview as 'clarity of expression, grasp of narrative and argument, reasoning ability, appreciation of different points of view, awareness and concern for socio-economic problems, ranges and depth of interests and personal attributes relevant to interaction with people'.

The interview phase is also known as the Personality Test. It is aimed at evaluating the candidate's personality, whether he is capable to be an able administrator or not. The applicant is assessed not only for his/her intellect but also for his/her overall personality development, his/her alertness, balance of judgement and qualities of honesty, integrity and leadership. Therefore, groundwork for the Interview needs proper planning. The committee members seek some attributes in the aspirant and decide whether he/she is able for a career in civil services or not. For being selected, the aspirant should have a positive approach, should have an attentive mind with quick reflexes, should be free from any sort of bias, should be good at making speedy decisions and should have the capability to act under stress and to handle difficult situations. Preparation for the Interview is a nonstop process. This includes a wide reading of books, journals, magazines and at least two newspapers. One should make an effort to develop his/her conversational skills with the right pronunciation. The aspirant should be ready to respond to questions on his background, hobbies and extra-curricular actions. The ideal way is to discuss current affairs and recent issues with friends. One worthy form of rehearsing possible questions would be to have mock interviews and discussion groups. The aspirant should self-analyse his/her strengths and weaknesses and make a sensible effort to play on his strengths.

Some Beneficial Guidelines for a Successful Interview at UPSC:

- To have a confident body language
- To have a good personal turnout and ensuring the right posture

- To answer questions clearly and positively
- Try to stay calm and composed even when faced with challenging questions
- Try answering to the point.

Points to be avoided at the UPSC Interview:

- Avoid the expression, 'I am sorry'.
- Avoid informal clichés like 'as you know', 'that's correct', 'of course', 'indeed', 'obviously' and so on.
- Avoid technical terminology. Nevertheless, if a member continues to assess you in any technical field, you can use technical terms.
- Maintain a cheerful outlook. Now and then you can appear serious, but most of the time keep smiling or look cheerful and composed. One caution here: if the committee members laugh, you should only smile. It is only when you keep some amount of distance that the board initiates to wonder about the depth of your personality.
- Avoid long introductions. Come straight to the point.
- Show human concern whenever possible in your answers.
- You have to be logically consistent and assess things rationally while talking. You need to defend what you say while giving due respect to the views of the board. Stop trying to defend an answer if it becomes difficult to do so logically and fairly.
- Do not make quick or sweeping generalizations.

As per the UPSC report, it has been witnessed that from 1979 onwards, 90 per cent of the aspirant who succeed to the interview round hover around the minimal percentage of 55 per cent that is prescribed for the test. However to be confident of a Class I service, one has to normally obtain about 58 per cent marks. It has been observed that only those securing 60 per cent and above are sure of bagging a service of their own choice. The data clearly reveal that the marks in the interview test play a big role in final selection of candidates. ❑❑❑

9

Sample Actual Questions Asked at UPSC Interview

- **'Don't you think you can serve your country better by remaining a doctor and treating poor patients? Why do you want to be a civil servant?'**

It is better to answer this question practically instead of emotionally saying that you want to serve the country, because even a doctor helps the people. A doctor from Kerala was asked this question and her reply was as follows: - 'Because I want to treat the primary malady that afflicts our country, which creates so many poor in India. As a doctor I can treat only secondary maladies'. She even presented exact statistics and ideas on a rubber plantation for poverty alleviation signifying that she had spent significant time and thoughts on her future plans. She was awarded a score of 85 per cent.

- 'What are the problems faced by wheat cultivators in your state?' an M.Sc. (Agriculture) student from Palanpur was once asked. 'The problem is not so much to do with agronomy but with the lack of a seed bank in Palanpur', came the reply. The candidate got 80 per cent score.

- 'Is there a law in physics, which is relevant to administration?' a law graduate was prompted. 'Yes. Newton's third law of motion: for every action there is an equal and opposite reaction'. He got a cool 80 per cent.

The above queries can offer you an idea of how significant questions are asked from your subjects even as they are not directly from the syllabus.

❑❑❑

10

Types of Questions Asked at the UPSC Interview

- ***Relating to your name.*** Any well-known personality who has a similar or same name or surname.
- ***Your career choice.*** Why you want to join the civil services.
- ***Your Hobbies.*** Why you follow such a hobby or questions related to your hobby. So research well on your hobby.
- ***Hot recent topics*** like the Bird Flu and Tamiflu, Office of Profit, Sahara airlines deal and the growing airlines, Terror attacks in India, India–US Nuclear deal, Commonwealth games, Saurav Ganguly, etc. Make it a habit to read and watch the news. If any headline has something to do with your subject, then specially revise those portions. For instance, if you are a veterinary doctor, Bird flu may go on to other animal diseases that can contaminate men. If you are an MBBS, then you may be asked regarding human-to-human spread of epidemics or any other epidemics and precautions. You may even be inquired about the influence of MNC or drug producers responsible for the spread of fear. If you are from an economy background, the same topic will swing towards the economic implications of the Bird flu.
- ***How you will be using your specific knowledge*** (like if you are a doctor, lawyer, engineer, etc.) in the services.
- ***Situational questions.*** Suppose if you were the collector/SP of Varanasi, what would be your step after the Bomb Blast?
- ***Choice of services.*** The order of your choice of services can raise questions too.
- ***About your institution and related.*** If you are from IIM, you may be asked about the rising salaries, and if from IGNOU, you may be asked questions about the topics related to Indira Gandhi and so on.

- ***From your form.*** You must go through the form you have filled because most questions will arise from there. If you have changed subjects, mentioned anything out of the way, watch out for questions on them. Interviewers take cue from the form you have filled.

❑❑❑

11

Important Interview Skills Needed to Clear IAS/IPS Interview

- **Initiate Your Interview Preparation from January Onwards**

  The most vital step is to initiate early while preparing for the interview stage. If you start preparing from the start of the year, you will automatically get at least 3 months to prepare yourself for the finale. I also suggest you to start preparing from one year in advance so that you get enough time.

- **Respect the Committee Members Who will Take Your Interview**

  After entering the interview room, it is important to pay due respect to the members who will take your interview. The committee will observe your mannerism and decide whether you will be fit or not. So take mannerism seriously.

- **Remember What You Wrote in Your Mains Exam**

  One can qualify for the interview only after he/she successfully clears the written mains exam. Therefore, while you give interview, you may be asked what you did in your mains. So remember and revise what you wrote there.

- **Have Positive Views in Your Mind**

  Having a positive mindset is must while going for an interview. Usually, it happens that negative thoughts would start coming to your mind. Specially, who are giving interview for the first time? So be positive and think right.

- **Give Importance to Your Language Skills**

  Your medium of the interview (English or Hindi) does not matter much. What matters is the command over the particular language.

- **Be Patient and First Listen than Speaking**

  Listening is more important to respond properly. So, it is best to listen completely and then answer rather interrupting when they are speaking.

- **Prepare for the Question Why You Want to Join IAS?**

  Prepare for the most usual question, that is, why you want to join IAS. This will be perhaps the first question that you have to answer. So prepare an honest reply beforehand. You will find it easy to answer.

- **Speak Truth and Do Not Lie Yourself**

  If you are face a situation where you find questions to be tough, then do not tell a lie. Never create a fake story to boost yourself. Just tell them truthfully, it does not really matters.

- **Be Confident and Talk to them not at them**

  Making eye contact is a must for effective communication. You should always look into their eyes and then talk. This is very basic interview tip for a civil service interview. Lack of eye contact lets them think that you do not have self-confidence.

- **For Serious Question Give a Serious Reply**

  Although you should give a smile and give answers laughingly, if you confront a serious question, then your answer should be serious too. You have to display them that you care about what they are asking.

- **Prepare what you will Say for Hobby Section**

  The question about your hobby is a very serious and common question in a civil service interview. You should answer this question in a light mood. The board members must get a chance to laugh at some point in time.

- **Prepare for Your Additional Subjects Seriously**

  The additional subjects that you will opt for the civil service exams will be a deciding factor in your success. Usually, it is observed that aspirants seem to neglect their additional subject. So when faced with the questions from the same, they are not prepared. Hence, do not neglect your additional subjects as they may put some tough questions from it.

- **Your Views Must be Unbiased and Reasonable**

  If you are asked any question that is political in nature, then your answer must be fair and balanced. You must not hold a partial view about a particular subject or topic. They must get a sense that you are very balanced in your approach.

- **Be aware about Current Affairs and Other Latest Developments**

  You will be quizzed about current affairs and state of the country. Hence, it is necessary to be updated with the things going around the world. You must know what is happening in the country and around the world.

- **Have deep Knowledge about your State, City and District**

  They may put some questions regarding the state, city and district you come from. So it is good to gain decent knowledge about the same. They would like to know how much you care about the country.

- **Have a Sound General Knowledge**

  Having a good general knowledge is always very important to attain success in any interview. You should know about some great personality from India and around the world.

- **Be Calm Even if they Say You Do Not Know about some Topic**

  If any situation arises where you are asked about a particular subject which you have less knowledge about, but you keep on giving some irrelevant answers. You should not show anger when they say that you do not know anything about the subject.

- **It is good to Admit You Don't Know**

  It is very important to develop a habit to admit your weaknesses. You should hesitate to give a frank answer that you do know about this subject. There is nothing wrong in admitting honestly.

- **Fetch Debates and Discussions from All India Radio and BBC Documentaries**

  This is more related to preparation. You can download debates and discussions from different sources present online. You can hunt many such website which are offering downloads.

- **Be sure to not Show Anger or Frustration if Rejected**

  After the complete discussion, if you get the feeling from the body language of the interviewers that you will not be selected, be sure not to show anger or frustration at them. Just take it on your side.

Do Not Give Up

Finally, if you fail to make it to the final list, then do not lose your heart. You can prepare for the second time. It is normal that candidates clear their interview in second or third attempt. So do not give up.

❑❑❑

12

Most Recommended Approach and Framework for UPSC Interview Preparation

Know About Yourself

1. What is your roll number?
2. Brief about yourself.
3. What is your height/weight/age etc.? (These questions are just an attempt to make you fumble....keep cool)
4. Convey the meaning of your name or surname.
5. Famous persons having same birthday or year.
6. What is the reason that motivates you to join civil services?
7. What is the reason behind preferring IAS or IPS or IFS?

Have Good Knowledge About Your College

1. Upgrade your knowledge about the branch of your graduation. Also refresh your alertness about recent developments in your branch.
2. Gather information regarding the university/institute where you are graduated from.
3. Gather facts about UPSC members, their service and cadre.
4. Also have a good knowledge about your optional subject.
5. Prepare the answer about choosing the specific subjects as optional.
6. Why you want to join IAS even after higher education? Don't you think you should contribute in your field of specialization? (If you have done post-graduation or Ph.D.)
7. Why do you not pursue research? (If you are from science background)

Have Deep Knowledge About Your Place

Gather deep information about your home state or state of residence, in the following sectors:

- History
- Politics
- Culture
- Tourism
- General statistics
- Recent developments and current affairs
- Personalities
- Development
- Social problems

Here are Some Example Questions

1. What is special about your place? (Village/city/district/state)
2. Tourist or historical places around your native place.
3. Tell me five positives and negatives about your place. (native place/district/state/place of graduation)
4. What are the major problems in your district/state?
5. Historical importance of your native place/any place in your city.
6. General statistics about your district/state–Population, population density, literacy, economic importance, health etc.
7. Famous personalities of your state and district (In the field of art, literature, sports, social workers and leaders).
8. List chief ministers of different states. (Especially North Eastern states)

Gather Complete Information About Your Hobbies

- Well-known people associated with the hobby
- Significance of your hobby

- Information about it in historical context
- Your accomplishments related your hobby
- Benefits of your hobby
- They may also ask some unexpected questions related to your sports interests. They may say 'Oh! You play volleyball, then I'll ask about basketball/cricket'. A sweet smile is sufficient to tackle such questions.

For instance, if your hobby is related to 'Reading Books', they may ask the following questions:

- What types of books you read, fiction/non-fiction?
- Name of the last book you read? Who is the author of that book? What that book is about? How is that book? Name other books of the same author?
- Tell us something about your favourite writer and why you like him/her?
- Who won Nobel (literature), Man Booker, DSC prize and Jnanpith award this year?
- Which sports/games you play?

For instance, if the candidate's answer is volleyball, he/she may be asked about the following:

1. National and international events in volleyball
2. Who won Olympics, world cup, etc.?
3. Different rules and regulations of volleyball
4. Terms regarding court size, net width and length, etc.
5. Which is your favourite position in volleyball?
6. Captain of Indian team
7. Top players of Indian team
8. Who is your favourite player? Why?
9. Recent developments in volleyball.

Opinion-Based Questions

Shape your view about diverse issues of national importance: some of the common issues are listed below:

1. Multi-party system vs. two-party system
2. Prime ministerial system vs. presidential system
3. Coalition politics- arguments for and against
4. Regional parties and their importance
5. Naxalism and Indian policy towards naxal control. What need to be done?
6. Rivers, river water sharing, river linking, river tribunals etc.
7. Basic concepts of statistics and their applications—mean, median, mode, AM, GM, HM, Standard deviation, coefficient of variation
8. Geography of your home state and district
9. Euthanasia/mercy killing
10. Honour killing and Khaps
11. Tribal issues and tribal development
12. Recent legislations and new policies
13. Politics of your home state
14. Water conservation and water harvesting with special focus to your state
15. Juvenile and juvenile justice
16. Capital punishment/ death penalty—arguments for and against and other related issues
17. Important wars of India e.g. Buxar, Panipat, Plassey, Anglo-Mysore, Anglo-Nepal, Anglo-Afghan, Indo-Pak, Indo-China etc.
18. Acts passed before independence—regulating acts, 1909 Act, 1919 Act, 1935 Act, etc.

19. Concept of left, right and centre
20. Communism, Socialism, Capitalism
21. Maoism, Marxism, Leninism
22. Communalism
23. Israel-Palestine problem. India's relation with Israel
24. Indo-China relations
25. Indo-Pak relations
26. Indo-US relations
27. Indo-Russia relations
28. Recent international developments
29. How to balance development and environmental protection
30. Development vs. environment
31. Sustainable development
32. Demand for new states: pros and cons
33. Small state vs. large state
34. Terrorism and measures to control terrorism in India
35. Poverty: causes for poverty, its estimation, measures to be taken
36. Corruption: causes, measures to control corruption
37. Biodiversity and its conservation
38. Mining, mining in forests, illegal mining and related issues
39. AFSPA: arguments for and against
40. Public-private partnership: pros and cons
41. Rural problems and rural development
42. Food security and related issues
43. Direct cash transfer: Pros and cons
44. What is lacking in sports administration in India?
45. Police reforms
46. Indian intelligence
47. FDI, inflation, import-export, etc.

48. Agricultural credit and agricultural insurance
49. Web regulation, social media (pros and cons), IT act, etc.
50. Famous writers and theatre personalities of your state
51. Pardoning power of president and its importance
52. Protection and promotion of regional languages
53. Environmental issues
54. Recent central govt. programmes/schemes, bills, ordinances, acts, policies, etc.

General Instructions

1. Do not try to cheat them. Be straight and modest.
2. If you are not confident about the answer, then tell them that 'this is the answer....but I'm not sure'. If you are not aware about the answer, but you are guessing, then tell them that it's a guess or ask for their permission to guess.
3. Be confident with whatever you say. Do not lie. Even if you lie, do it confidently.
4. Smiling face is always a plus point (it indicates you are not nervous)
5. Do not talk negative. Be optimistic. Show that you have constructive thinking.
6. Do not get excited. Keep calm. Do not lose your patience.
7. Interview should not be taken as a question-answer session. It is a friendly and healthy discussion.

Point of View regarding Interview Enrichment Programme by an Interview Expert

The personality test or the interview being the final phase in the selection process in civil services examination is really important as it plays a big role in deciding the final merit. But at the same time, it is capable of bringing (or even to most of us who could not make it to the final list, it in fact does bring) disappointments as well.

The personality test carries 300 marks out of the total 2300 mark scheme of the Civil Services Examination based on which the final selection list is prepared. Like the Essay (that has 200 marks), the success and rank of a candidate is considerably determined by this small but important segment.

Regrettably, it is not observed very seriously by most of the candidates. It is very depressed to recognize that by the time these candidates get to recognize about its significance, it is already too late (i.e. when they do not discover their names in the list of successful candidates even though they have scored quite well in the main examination). That experience in fact is very painful one. It hurts us a lot, as all our hard earned efforts of significantly long time (i.e. from P.T days to the main till the interview and those long lived moments of dream) all vanish or get shattered in a moment. Not many candidates have managed to score over 100 marks according to the statistics of the 2009 main results. There have been an astonishingly high number of double-digit scores on the final list, as compared to the allotted interview scores. But this does not mean that there is not much possibility to overcome the obstacles of interview or it cannot be strategically prepared and scored well.

The nature of Interview for the Civil Services is unlike the other services interviews. The aspirants appearing for Civil Services are going to be quizzed by a Board who will have before them a record of their career. They will be quizzed on subjects of general interest regarding national and international importance. The aim of the interview is to test the personal aptness of the candidate for a career in public service by a Board of competent and unbiased members who themselves are generally bureaucrats having extensive experiences of this services.

The test aims to evaluate the mental ability of an aspirant. In extensive terms, this is in fact a review of not only his intellectual state but also social traits and his interests in current affairs. Some of the qualities to be judged are mental alertness, critical powers of assimilation, clear and logical exposition, balance of judgments, variety and depth of interests, ability for social cohesion and leadership, intellectual and moral integrity and so on.

The method of the interview is not that of a strict cross-questioning but of a normal, though directed and purposive conversation which aims to judge the mental qualities of the aspirant. The interview test is not intended to be a test either of the specialized or general knowledge of the candidates which has been already tested through their written papers. Aspirants are anticipated to have taken an intelligent interest not only in their chosen subjects of academic study but also in the happenings which are occurring around them both within and outside their own state or country as well as in modern currents of thought and in new findings which should awake the curiosity of well-educated youth.

So here, one is expected to be diplomatic in taking up a stand and handling the issues in specifically designed/created conditions or hypothetical conditions by the interviewers during the process of interview. The exactness of language, discipline of thought and lot of endurance in placing the views are the fundamentals. Remember! Your entire personality is going to be judged on every single word that one happens to speak. Therefore, one needs to be extra careful about choosing the words during the process of personality test. The personality test requires the candidates to exhibit not only the art of balanced and precise thoughts, but also the art of delivering them or communicating them effectively. This plainly indicates towards the requirement of a good tactic through experienced guidance and practice in right direction that's all. There are candidates who have scored 240 plus marks in 2009 examination, and most of the toppers and rank holders attain advantage in interview scores only. Therefore, RIAS has devised INTERVIEW ENRICHMENT PROGRAMME for CSE, which is scientifically created to help not only Delhi-based regular students but also those who cannot come to Delhi for different reasons. It aims to harness and complement those vital components of the interview so as to improve the overall scores of distant and diversely placed participants.

❑❑❑

13

Significance of Comprehending the Phenomenon and Process of IAS/IPS Interview: Role of Communication Skills, Body Language, Time Management and Stress Management

The IAS interviews can be one of those special experiences that one can never forget in one's life. Being one of the most prestigious and elite services available so far not only in India but the world over, CSE interviews constitute a wide, diverse and a general understanding of literally everything under the sun. Therefore, it demands maturity, humility, rationality, communicability, humbleness, presence of mind and of course, the extensive knowledge base. The knowledge criterion however, is already checked during main examination time, but rest of these things must be reflected in the personality test so that you are given good amount of marks which is decisive in your final ranking and success. Abraham Lincoln, one of the most influential presidents of USA, has said, 'If I was given six hours to chop a tree, I would spend the first four sharpening the axe'. This saying suggests how good interview preparation for exams like IAS can bring changes in one's life. The session of your interview may be for twenty minutes, thirty minutes or an hour, but you need to prepare yourself for much longer duration.

Usually, it is going to be 35 minutes or so, but don't worry they would appear as if you spent just few seconds. By preparing ahead of an ensuing interview, you have given yourself a distinct advantage. Many of the aspirants develop a belief that they are smart enough to tackle the interview successfully and there is no need for specific preparation for an interview. However, this belief turns to be fallacious and they do not fare as well in the interview as they should have after through preparation. This happens not because of their lack of competence but because of lack of their right mental framework in the interview process. This can only be sharpened when one undergoes with practices. Yes, amount of practice may vary from person to person depending upon one's personality, maturity, education and exposure. Therefore, practice is essential for a confident and high mark fetching interviews.

Thus, need for specific preparation for an interview becomes obvious. Once an eminent army general said, If you shed more sweat in peace, you will have to shed less blood in a battle'. What is true for a battle is true for an interview too. Therefore, keep yourself fully prepared before you face an interview. This preparation will help you in two ways. First you will never feel surprised or awkward even if you face any unexpected question from the interviewers. Second, when you have prepared yourself fully, you develop confidence within you. Due to this confidence, you can do far better as compared to a situation when you have not prepared yourself fully.

Try to Understand Yourself Fully

For any individual, it is desirable that he/she comprehends him/herself completely before taking up any new activity. Interview being a new and a different activity, it is desirable that you know yourself fully. One Chinese philosopher has said long back, 'the most crucial problem with us is that we don't know ourselves fully. With the result, either we overestimate or underestimate us'. In fact, psychologically, one's total personality defined in a broad sense having technical (academic) and behavioural competences can be divided into four quadrants as depicted in the figure below:

	Known to self	Not known to self
Known to others	Open	Blind
Not known to others	Hidden	Unknown

As seen in the figure above, all the four quadrants are in equal size just to begin with. In real practice, the size of each quadrant varies from one individual to another. Those individuals who analyse themselves on continuous basis and improve accordingly are able to increase the size of the first quadrant; those who do not do it are unable to increase it. Let us discuss these quadrants in short.

1. ***Open:*** Open quadrant of one's personality is that part about which an individual concerned is aware but at the same time, those who interact with her are also aware about it. In reality, it represents that part of personality which is used very often. For instance, extroversion/introversion, openness/closeness, emotional maturity/immaturity and the like are quite frequently known to self as well as to others.
2. ***Blind:*** This part of personality is known to others but is not known to self. For instance, an individual behaves in a particular way but he/she is not fully aware about why he/she has behaved in a particular way but others can point out the reason for this particular behaviour. This is due to the fact that a person copies behaviours of others either consciously or sub-consciously. His/her conduct is affected by both conscious and sub conscious minds but he/she can identify the reasons of an action based on his/her conscious mind while the action based sub-conscious mind is not explainable.
3. ***Hidden:*** Hidden quadrant of one's personality is that part about which the person herself is aware about but others are not aware. This happens in two situations: first, the person uses that personality characteristics very rarely in her behaviour pattern and, therefore, others cannot form exact opinion about this part of personality. Second, the person herself may try to hide this part of personality as people learn to hide many of their ideas and feeling right from childhood.
4. ***Unknown:*** Unknown quadrant of personality is neither known to the person concerned nor to others in a given time frame. In fact, people's qualities are like an iceberg. An iceberg floats on the water surface. Only its ten per cent part is visible while

remaining ninety per cent part remains under water which is not visible. In a case of a person, what is seen above the person surface is only small part of the qualities. Large part of the qualities which is known as potential is hidden below the surface. Such qualities come on surface when the person faces a crisis which comes in the way of achieving her valued goals. For instance: a person runs with his fastest speed when a barking dog starts running behind him/her.

On the basis of the above discussion, you can evaluate your qualities. For doing this, divide your total qualities in two parts – technical qualities and behavioural qualities. So far your qualities falling in quadrant 3 are concerned, you are fully aware about these and you can assess yourself on your own. About qualities falling in quadrant 2, you are not fully aware about these. Therefore, you can take the help of your well-wishers who know you fully like you parents, trusted friends, etc. Assessing qualities falling in quadrant 4 is problematic. For this purpose, you can recall your experiences of handling crises and what you really did in those circumstances. For example, assess how much efforts you put in preparing yourself for the Civil Services examination. This will reveal how hard working you are in case situation demands, which of course it does; I am sure you agree to this. You may have various qualities but not necessary in equal proportion. Some of your qualities may be outstanding while some may not be of this level. Therefore, define the degree to which you possess various qualities. For this purpose, either you may use 3- point scale: very good (3) good (2), or average (1) or 5-point scale: outstanding (5) very good (4) good (3) and average (2) and below average (1). Whatever scale you use, use it for evaluating all your qualities. This will depict the comparison among various qualities in an easy manner.

As your academic (technical) and behavioural qualities are in different forms, pinpoint all these forms. For instance, your technical qualities may pertain your proficiency in different subjects that you might have studied at different levels of your education. You might be outstanding in some but not necessarily that much outstanding in others. Do not assess yourself simply on the basis of marks scored in examination but assess yourself in the light of your view. You can do this exercise in your mind or you can write your exercise on a piece of paper. Completing this exercise on a piece of paper is more desirable at the early stage because when you award a particular grade to a particular quality possessed by you, you think more logically before awarding the grade.

In case you do this exercise in your mind, you are likely to follow a generalized approach and your evaluation may not be as objective as you wish. When you undertake exercise of assessing your qualities and writing the result of this assessment on a piece of paper, it will look like the table given below. In the table, only limited number of qualities has been presented. You can increase the number of qualities up to any level depending on your requirements. While assessing your various qualities, you have honesty of the highest order so that you have realistic assessment of yourself. Do not hesitate to award grade – 1 (average) to a quality that you do not possess above this level. After all, you are doing this exercise for yourself and are not going to disclose its results to others so that they become aware about your shortcomings. This approach of evaluating your qualities honestly will assist you in two ways:

1. On doing this exercise honestly, you become aware about your shortcomings and you can take necessary steps to overcome these shortcomings. It is worth-noting that different qualities are not in-born but these are acquirable. You can achieve that by taking relevant steps.
2. In case you are completely aware about your qualities, you can consider your outstanding qualities as your strengths if a question is asked associated with this aspect (this is often asked in an IAS interview).

Practice Standard Questions

When preparing for examination, some students inculcate the habit of writing answers of standard questions and assess whether they can complete answering required number of questions within the fixed time. In the light of this practice, they try to overcome their deficiency if there is any. In the same way, you can rehearse standard questions likely to be asked in the interview. This process will give you confidence as you will be able to eliminate any deficiency that you experience during this process. For rehearsing standard questions, it is desirable that sit on chair located at a place which does not have any kind of disturbance. Sit In a composed manner as if you are sitting for an interview. If desired by you, hang a large-sized mirror on the wall facing you. This will help you in observing your body language during the process of rehearsing questions. After setting the above environment, you ask a question to yourself and give answer of this. You may ask a question by uttering words or by thinking in your mind. However, while giving its answer, utter words in tone, speed and loudness as if you are actually sitting in the interview. This practice will help you in overcoming deficiency that you may come across during the process. For practicing standard questions, usually, two questions come in the mind of prospective interviewee:

1. How much time should be fixed for a single rehearsing session?
2. How many sessions are required for rehearsal?

The answers of these questions are that no fixed time duration is there for a single rehearsal session and number of sessions as these differ from one person to another. Some persons take more time for getting prepared fully for the interview while other takes lesser time. However, that much time should be used which is sufficient to prepare for an interview fully. In this backdrop, you can decide time duration for a single rehearsal session along with the number of sessions.

For this purpose, you can take the help of some of the interviews of successful candidates either in written form or in the recorded form of mock interviews that are available with many reputed IAS coaching centres, which if requested can be obtained easily. By going through these interviews carefully, you must have been in a position to understand that how good, non-controversial and balanced interviews are delivered within the precise word limits and suitable languages. Use this experience for your own evaluation i.e. after the end of a session; evaluate yourself whether you have achieved commensurate proficiency required. These self-practiced exercises will be of immense help to you in facing the actual interview successfully. If your self-evaluation indicates that you have achieved the required proficiency, you can stop the process because beyond this level, this process will not contribute much. In case your self-evaluation shows that you have any type of deficiency, you must repeat this process till you acquire the proficiency needed.

Take Part in Mock Interviews that are Interactive

It is essential that you go through some sessions of mock interviews before going for the real interview. A mock interview is the duplication or simulation of an actual interview. Therefore, it is conducted in a same way as actual interview is conducted. The basic objective of a mock interview is to give an interviewee feeling of an actual interview. This feeling emerges because the mock interview is conducted on similar conditions or creating the similar environment to that of the UPSC. In order to make the mock interview effective, it is essential that the mock interview is conducted in a way in which the real interview is conducted, both in terms of physical setting as well as interviewers. It is understandable that actual match is very difficult but some reputed institutions are having such facilities. But you got to be careful in choosing them. As many coaching institutes in Delhi and elsewhere shall be eager to provide interview guidance as and when the main result is out, even if they are not competent enough. The reason is two one, they tend to make quick money and the second, they cash in some of the bio-data which can be matched when the final results are out and they shall appear with the claim of being the guide of such candidates. Well, physical setting includes furnishing of interview room on the pattern of room meant for real interview. So far as interviewers are concerned, you have two options. First, you may take the help of any competent interview service provider. However, this may be little difficult to establish but you got to ensure that. Second, you may take the help of your parents/ guardians/relatives, friends, or even classmates for this purpose. In such a case, you can have more mock interview sessions depending on your requirements without much waste of time and money. At the time of mock interview, make an attempt to overcome some of the mistakes usually made by interviewees.

These can be listed as follows:

1. ***Lack of Good First Impression:*** Many interviewees fail to make good first impression. This happens because of lack of confidence, lack of preparation, and facing such an occasion for first time. Since first impression becomes last impression in many cases of interview, it is essential that you overcome your inhibition if there is any, so that you are able to make good first impression. If required, you may undertake more than one mock interview sessions.
2. ***Practicing Certain Words Too often:*** Some interviewees repeat certain words like 'it is nothing but…, 'I mean that…, 'I feel that..., 'according to me…, etc. repeating such words quite frequently by an interviewee during the interview process creates bad impressions in the mind of the interviewers. Therefore, try to avoid uttering such words beyond the required proposition.
3. ***Wrong Body Language:*** Usually, body language in any oral communication is first followed by spoken language like English, Hindi, etc. Body language also supports spoken words during the entire communication process. Body language consists of facial expression, movements of various parts of the body, and physical posture during the interview process. Many interviewees fail to use appropriate body language during interview. With the result, whatever they communicate does not become effective. So, it is necessary that you synchronize your body movement as per your spoken language at the time of mock interviews.
4. ***Inhibition:*** Many interviewees exhibit inhibition at the time of the interview. In the interview process, an interviewer may ask a question which has not been understood by the interviewee correctly or not understood at all. In such a case,

the interviewee should request the interviewer to repeat the question but the interviewee fails to do so because of his unfounded inhibition. With the result, either he gives wrong answer or shows his ignorance about the answer. Both these options are unfavourable for the interviewee.

Evaluating Result of Mock Interview

Once the mock interview is completed, it is necessary that its result is assessed so that deficiency, if any, is avoided. While evaluating the result of mock interview, treat it as real interview. The result should be evaluated by yourself as well as by the interviewers. It is better that first you evaluate your own performance in the mock interview and subsequently ask feedbacks from the interviewers. In assessing yourself in mock interview, you should try asking the following questions to yourself and answer these in yes or no.

- Was I enthusiastic enough?
- Did I let the interviewers begin the interview?
- Did I maintain a good posture during the interview?
- Did I maintain proper eye contact when I spoke?
- Did I listen to questions carefully and, if necessary, ask the interviewers to repeat the questions or to be more specific?
- Did I express myself vividly and use appropriate language?
- Did I take time to think before answering the questions?
- Was I able to be calm, control my nervousness and exhibit self-confidence?
- Did I give positive answers by giving stress on my strengths and skills?
- Did I answer questions as honestly as possible?

In case the answers of above questions are in yes, your performance can be regarded as good. If the answer of any of the above questions is in no, try to analyse why it is so and try coming out of the deficiency. So far, your evaluation is based on your own perception about your performance. To verify it, take the feedback from the interviewers.

If their feedback matches your self-evaluation, the thing is alright. If there is difference between two sets of evaluation, get the feedback from the interviewers where you have gone wrong. Have a joint session with the interviewers to evaluate feedback. During this process, it is possible that the interviewers may criticize some of your ideas/positions during the mock interview process. Take such criticism positively and with open mind. If they offer some advices, take them seriously and improve yourself in the light of those. Even if your friends or classmates have acted as the interviewers, do not show any resentment because that will go against the basic philosophy of learning. While doing the evaluation, if you find a number of shortcomings, try to get rid of these shortcomings one by one and take another mock interview session after a gap of a few days to assess the improvement you have made during the period.

Try Avoiding Common Mistakes at the Time of the Interview

Some mistakes which are committed by candidates at the time of interview either knowingly or unknowingly can be avoided. Some of these mistakes which have significant impacts on interview outcomes like lack of good first impression, repeating certain words too frequently, use of inappropriate body language and inhibition etc. which have been already discussed above. Some more mistakes committed during interview process are listed here. Such mistakes may not seem to be significant prima facie but these are likely to decrease your chance of being successful.

You can abide by the following guidelines to avoid such mistakes:

1. Avoid taking your cell phone inside the interview room. If you have to carry it inside the interview room, put it in off mode. Ringing of a cell phone distracts attention which is not liked by anyone and may be considered in all probability, as offensive by those aged person.

2. Do not show nervousness at the time of interview. Do some exercise/yoga/meditation to get rid of your nervousness before the interview.

3. Do not talk unnecessary about your qualities too much. Let your qualities speak about you themselves. If you happen to brag about your qualities too much, it will raise expectations of the interviewers and they would evaluate you against those raised expectations which can prove disastrous for you at the end, and it is not fair also.
4. Do not check time by looking at your wrist watch during the interview process. This is a sign of low confidence.
5. Do not tell a lie at any stage of the interview. In cross checking, it will be revealed and will go against you.
6. Do not make any adverse comment on the facilities provided or about the mode of communication to the UPSC etc. during any point in the interview process, remember all these are secondary stuff.
7. If you are already in job (govt. or private) or are selected in allied (or inferior, for you) services, do not start criticizing your current employer/organization. In the same way, there should not be any criticism of your academic institution or persons related to it. In fact, criticism of any type is taken as a negative approach and is not appreciated.
8. Do not show any type of fidgetiness even if your interview is not proceeding on the line of your expectation. Try to bring the situation back according to your expectation by overcoming those obstacles which has caused this phenomenon/situation and if you cannot, they themselves would do; just keep the patience. They sometimes check your mindfulness and patience during unfavourable and tough times. So take it in that spirit.
9. Do not show any clue, either verbal or non-verbal, that you are very much disparate for this career. Desperation of any kind is not liked. If you do well in the interview, you will be offered the position.
10. In case you are not clear about any issue/question asked to you or do not know it at all, then be honest and express it or rather accept it with humility giving a gentle smile saying 'I do not know sir'.

People usually hesitate to accept their shortcomings and try give wild guesses or even try to bluff them. But dear, you should remember that they are very experienced bureaucrats (mostly) and have seen much of the world than you did, so you cannot be fool them or even bluff them. Therefore, better try not for such ideas however good it may appear to you; just check such instincts/ emotions.

Body Language(s) Required for the Interview

Body language is an important component of oral communication. In reality, when we communicate orally to someone, our body language speaks much earlier than our words. For example, the interviewers may perceive your behaviour on the basis of the manner you enter the interview room. Therefore, understanding of how you can reinforce your spoken words through your body language is very important. Body language consists of gestures (movement of different parts of body), postures (body positions), and facial expressions by which a person manifests various physical, mental, and emotional states and communicates non-verbally (without using any word) with others. In some instances, communication takes place through body language alone. Look at how dumb communicate among themselves without using a word; how a news-reader conveys news meant for dumb without using a single word; how a Bharatanatyam dancer conveys the meanings through her actions using different parts of her body. In the case of an interview, body language can stand alone, for example, when you are answering a question, you can make out easily by looking at the facial expression of the interviewer whether he is happy with your answer or not. However, in the interview, body language is also combined with spoken words from both sides' interviewers and interviewees. When both of these are combined, they put emphasis on certain things that is, differentiating things that are more important than others which are usual.

Put Negative Body Language(s) at Bay

While following positive body language is significant, it is equally significant to overcome negative body language at the time of an interview. Taking guard against negative body language is required because in many cases, body language emerges from one's subconscious mind. Therefore, you are required to know negative body language so that you can take precautions against them. In general, the following aspects of body language are negative and may emerge unknowingly. Fidgets like playing with one's hair, touching or rubbing chin or nose frequently, biting nails, pulling or tugging of ear, rubbing back of head or neck, moving palm on the table top, clicking ball pens or likes etc. give impression of nervousness. In fact very often people use fidgets to overcome their nervousness. So, keep a watch on all these. Many wrong body gestures and postures like looking at the interview room decoration or other eye-catching elements, avoiding eye contact, waving foot, hands clasped behind back, palms closed, etc. give an indication that you lack preparedness and interest. All these postures have to be kept at bay.

Start of the Interview

When it is your turn for the interview, you will be called by the interviewers. A person who has been given the responsibility of calling the candidates will inform you. On this call, collect all your materials (you must have put all these materials in your folder) and proceed towards the interview room. If the door of the room is open, ask the permission from the interviewers by asking gently, 'May I come in sir?' enter the room only after the permission is granted. This permission may be either verbal (through words) or gesture (through indication). Walk confidently to the seat meant for the interviewee and wish the interviewers by saying 'Good morning madam/sir', or 'Good afternoon' as the case may be. Do not sit on the chair unless you are asked to do so. In most of the cases, one of the interviewers says the candidate to occupy the seat. In some cases, the interviewers wish to test the etiquette and manner of an interviewee and delay deliberately in saying her/him to occupy the seat. If this happens with you, ask gently to occupy the seat. After you occupy the seat the interview will begin. A typical interview is divided into three phases: establishing rapport, gathering relevant information, and closing. Normally, the interviewers follow this sequence in the interview. All these phases are completed in a single sitting. In report-establishing-phase, the interview panel tries to establish rapport with the candidate so that he is able to give complete information about himself and his worth related to job requirements. Beginning of this phase is made by briefly reading bio-data of the candidate normally by the chairman of the panel or any interviewer who has been assigned this task. During the period when your bio-data is being read, listen to carefully and nod your head in yes if it is being read correctly. If there is any mistake (may be because of an error committed by the typist while preparing copies of your bio-data required by the interviewers, or by oversight of the reader, or mistake committed by the reader deliberately to test your proficiency), interrupt the reader immediately but politely. Your action will be taken positively by the interviewers as it shows your attentiveness. If you wait for the reader to finish his reading, the interviewers will take it negatively as they may perceive that you are not quite attentive. However, this practice of interruption should not be adopted during question answer session. After completing reading of you bio-data, the interviewers may ask you informational questions as well. In some cases, the interviewers may choose to put some information questions like the place of your residence, mode of journey from your place to interview place, or similar such questions of this nature before going through reading of your bio-data in order to establish better rapport. After establishing rapport with you, the interviewers will move to next phase of the interview. In this phase, the interviewers will make an attempt to solicit as much information as possible from you to judge your suitability as a good administrator, both technically as well as behaviourally. In this phase, questions related to the technical and behavioural aspects are asked. Technical aspect will include your graduation subjects to whatever professional or higher academic achievements you have made. It may also relate to your optional subjects for both P.T as well as Main examination. So, You must undergo a brief brush-up done beforehand.

Usually, this phase requires maximum time out of the total time assigned for the interview. After finishing information gathering phase, the interviewer proceeds to last phase of the interview that is, closing phase. After probing you to the required level, the interviewers may ask questions of national and international importance, which are generally from the current affairs or happenings during the time or even before. They may ask you to give your opinion or take a stand on certain issues. There you got to be extra careful and this where the Mock interview guidance come in handy. After all these get over, the panel chairman indicates about closing the interview session by wishing the candidates. While coming out of the interview, move out keeping gentle smiles and thank and greet them for the last time.

Interpersonal Skills

Communication skills refer to one's ability to express one's views and listen to other's views effectively. The first rule is to be a good listener. It is not found frequently in practice. Candidates are always found to be eager in talking or giving answers. But one should know that the answers become relevant only when you have responded correctly to whatever has been asked to you not what you know or think on something else. So first of all inculcate the habit of paying attention to what people have to say then only one should try to respond through introspections. Well, couple of points for how you should make your responses. You should be very careful in choosing the words in whatever language you happen to speak on, as couple of words here and there and the meanings change. So always speak your minimal, try to be as precise as you can but at the same time be clear at you exposition. If you are well prepared you could also use persuasive communication. Persuasive communication aims at persuading others to see a problem from multiple perspectives and try to press to the point you are more comfortable about. Remember most of the times your interview is guided by what you have answered. Most of the questions would arise from what you have answered already. So, with persuasive communication you can more or less devise the course of your interview. But, this needs through practice and adequate preparation. Therefore, you should prepare yourselves well for the interview.

Skills Associated with Problem Solving

Problem-solving skills refer to evolving solutions to a problem or set of problems. A problem is a gap between desired state of affair and actual state of affair at a particular point of time. With a purpose to overcome this gap, relevant action is needed. For identifying this action, problem-solving skills are needed. Problem-solving skills are relevant not only for case-based group discussion as widely perceived but are relevant to topic-based group discussion too. Your problem-solving skills will be reflected in your following actions during group discussion process. While discussing a topic or case, adopt systems approach, that is, treat the topic/case as a system and identify its different components (technically called subsystems) and their interrelationships. For instance, if you are talking about status of education in India, classify education into three categories: primary education, secondary education and higher education; these three categories of education have high relationships – a higher-level education is dependent on a lower-level education to a great extent.

With a purpose to determine issues involved in topic/case, apply your creative power. Through this power, you can detect root causes underlying issues. For instance, while discussing the reasons for poor status of education in India, do not just mention lack of funds, lack of discipline in the society, etc. These may not be primary causes but intervening causes resulted from root causes, for example, lack of commitment on the part of concerned governments or similar such causes. While suggesting a solution to any problem, check its feasibility and its effect on other components of the system, otherwise, it is likely that your solution may solve one problem but may generate more problems. If possible, also see how your solution can be implemented. For instance, if you mention that governments should assign more funds to education, also mention from where these funds should come as governments usually come across scarcity of funds.

Skills that are to be Evaluated

As discussed previously, UPSC is giving high importance to those candidates who have skills relevant to becoming good team players. These skills include problem-solving skills, human skills, communication skills, initiative and leadership skills. These are known as core skills for a good administrator. This is the reason why these skills are being included and checked right from the preliminary levels which is reflected in the new Preliminary syllabus-2011. These are also reflected in last year's main examination. Evaluators focus on these skills while evaluating performance of candidates during the personality test as well. Therefore, you need to imbibe these attributes through extensive mock practices with your behaviour and your attentiveness.

❑❑❑

14

Preparing for Personality Test at an IAS Interview: Role of Character and Decision-Making

Vital Instructions

- The process of interview is nowadays called Personality Test.
- The reason for the same is that it is not a test of knowledge, but of the overall character of the candidate/aspirant.
- Interview is mainly a psychological test that is just content-based. Besides good communicative skills and self-confidence, good knowledge base surely gives you an upper hand.
- However, it is recognized that almost all the aspirants in the Personality Test initiate more or less as equals in the sphere of knowledge base.
- The most significant fact to know about an interview is that it is not always a question-answer session and that the committee members are constantly searching for various aspects of one's personality.
- As an individual is expected to know everything under the sun, if you do not know the answer to a particular question, do not hesitate to say I don't know with a reasonable amount of cheerfulness.
- Remember your knowledge has been thoroughly tested during the earlier stages of the Prelims and Mains.
- Personality is an asset that evolves and changes every day.

Preparation

- Have a photocopy of the form filled for the Mains examination. Most of the early questions, namely, the meaning of your name, educational background, professional experience, hobbies, etc. will be asked from this form only. Make an attempt to prepare your bio-data; approximately 70% questions are based on bio-data, 20% questions are based on your subject and 10% are based on current affairs.

- Candidates should take an intelligent interest not only in subjects of their specialization, but also in general awareness.
- Have a good insight into your interests and hobbies as there will be a few questions regarding your levels of knowledge as regards your hobbies and interests.
- Have a good knowledge about your hometown and home state. If you are from a place of historical importance or tourist interest, prepare well on it.
- It is very important to know yourself. Prepare brief answers to choice of your subjects, family background and meaning of your name. You should make an attempt to take the lead by answering questions based on your bio-data.
- One of the ideas of triumph is to prepare for the Personality Test simultaneously with the written test.
- If an individual presents himself as a bookworm, the probability of his/her selection is reduced. The candidate must exhibit an all-round personality, which indicates that the aspirant possesses a complete personality.

Mock Practice

- The best idea is to make a group of 4 to 5 people, as the groundwork for Personality Test cannot be done in isolation. Try undertaking as many mock interviews as possible.
- No coaching centre can develop/transform your personality in a matter of few days. However, some guidance may help in removing some weaknesses/grey areas and can provide a platform for a well-planned preparation and group discussions.
- Undertake mock interviews. In it, ask your friends to grill you so that you can cope with the pressure from the Board easily.

- Discuss a lot with your friends. This not only aids in assimilating different points of view, but also in improving knowledge levels.

Dressing Up

- Dressing sense is also important. The choice of dress should be as per the weather conditions. Do not wear newly stitched clothes, as they might make you uneasy. Light colours should be preferred. White colour is a good choice.
- Going with comfortable clothes is a good option. Men should go for light-coloured shirt and a dark trouser with a tie (if weather permits). Women should don a saree or salwar/kameez.
- It is important to pay attention to the minute details like ironed dress, polished shoes, hair accessories, trimmed nails, etc. Polish your footwear meticulously. Use convenient footwear like black or brown leather shoes.
- Women aspirants should take extra care to avoid the hair falling over the face as it could annoy both you and the interviewer.
- Beware wearing anything that relates you with a religious or political group.
- Do not use heavy perfume/deodorants.
- In case you have cold and a running nose, carry a handkerchief, or sufficient stock of tissue paper. Tissue paper is preferable.
- Some aspirants take medicine to remain relax on the previous night of the interview; this is not a good habit as the effect of medicine may lower your alertness during the interview.
- Your eating habit may take a toll on you. Have a light meal on the day of the Personality Test. Do not go for the interview with an empty stomach. However, also avoid over-eating, or having a heavy meal.
- First impression is often the best impression. So create a positive, good impression within the first few minutes of the interview.

Entry

- Try and reach 20 to 30 minutes early. Prepare a route map and arrive well in time so that you can get enough time to relax.
- While you wait for your turn in the waiting area, read a newspaper or a magazine and try to remain relaxed without thinking too much of what will happen in the interview. Try not to presuppose situations.
- Be calm and composed and do not get nervous when you are waiting for your turn. While waiting, try relaxing with closed eyes and practice deep breathing. It really relaxes you.
- Take a final, deep breath before entering the boardroom.
- Do remember to knock at the door before entering, as it indicates basic courtesy.
- After entering the room, greet all the members cordially and do not try to sit down without being asked to.
- If there is a lady member in the interview board, greet her first.
- Be mindful of your body language when you are seated.
- Men are preferred to keep the feet flat on the floor during the interview, knees at waist level, and hands on your thighs and place your elbows on the armchair. Avoid locking hands.
- Women can cross ankles or legs, but keep the bottom leg straight down and over the top leg and keep your elbows positioned on the arms of the chair.
- When the committee members thank you at the end of the Personality test, do not forget to thank the members one last time with straight body posture at the time of leaving the room.
- You should know that interview is a two-way process.
- Be at ease. Be yourself during the interview. Your goal should be to make the committee members comfortable in your presence. Be truthful, transparent and predictable.
- Majority of the questions asked in the Interview are opinion-based.

- Don't expect any expression on the faces of board members, even if your answer is very good.

At Time of Interview

1. During interview, how you say what you say is more important. It is the style of presentation that matters.
2. Your personality is, on an average, judged in 25 to 30 minutes. Hence, it is your responsibility to present your best in front of the board.
3. Be alert and pay attention to each question carefully. Try not to jump into an answer before the complete question has been posed as you will end up wasting time on answering a question that you were not actually asked. If you are not sure of what was asked, you can always courteously look for a clarification.
4. Take your time before initiating to answer the question. Think over the question, take your time and organize the broad outline of the answer before airing it. Pause a while before answering, even if you know the answer.
5. At times, you will be given circumstances wherein you will be needed to take a decision. In such conditions, the board is assessing your skill to understand issues and use reason and good judgement logically, precisely and reach at a balanced decision.
6. Your answers should be crisp and to the point. Do not stretch it too long.
7. Maintain a gentle smile off and on during the Personality Test without overdoing it. It shows a sense of ease and confidence. Wherever possible, use your sense of humour judiciously.

Do's and Don'ts

- It is of utmost importance to give respect to board members as they are usually very senior and learned people.
- Don't go by any stories/rumours spread by others. Avoid unnecessary details.

- Don't ask the previous aspirant about his/her interview.
- The board is not partial towards anyone.
- Never make any sweeping statements/generalized descriptions.
- Form habit to accept your mistakes boldly.
- Speak honestly, truthfully and modestly.
- Do not give a hasty reply.
- Always maintain eye contact with the Board members while answering.
- Be polite and courteous.
- Don't argue with the board.
- Stay on your views. Don't change your views just because the Board doesn't agree with the same.
- Never try to present a made-up appearance or politically correct replies.
- You should have the ability to justify your views.
- Have tea or coffee, if any member proposes the same to you. This will portray that you are relaxed and it will also help in lightening and relaxing further proceedings and give them an informal touch.
- Avoid chewing gums and other munching items as it gives a negative and a careless image.
- Practise mock interviews in front of a mirror. Look out for unnecessary actions/emotions and try to correct any shortcomings. If possible record your own answers and play them again for finding out errors.
- Don't condemn any government policies or even individuals.
- Take a good sleep in the night before interview. A good, sound sleep will help you in being refreshed, cheerful and relaxed. Otherwise you will have a fuzzy head and you will betray a confused personality. You will neither be able to understand questions correctly, nor be able to think clearly.

- Do not speak speedily. Speak slowly and clearly so that the Board can understand what you are saying and do not have to interrupt you or ask you to repeat your views.
- The Board will assess you for qualities such as honest and integrity, logical exposition, balance of judgment, leadership skills, mental alertness, variety and depth of interest, social cohesion, moral integrity, acumen, your reaction to a weird situation, your views on diverse topics.
- Sometime, the committee members might make pressure upon you. You should not panic as it is a strategy aimed at gauging the point till which you can preserve your cool under pressure and can think originally even in pressure cooker conditions. Try to resemble tealeaves show your true colours when in hot waters.
- Frame your views on matters in a logical and rational way backed by data whenever necessary.
- To remain aware about the recent happenings/events nationally and internationally, aspirants should read magazines and newspapers (at least two for interview) and follow current affairs-based television shows.
- Think that all questions are asked with a good reason and answer them accordingly.
- Carry a file/folder to keep your certificates and documents in an organized manner. They are verified before you enter the interview room (you don't need to carry file/folder inside board room). ❑❑❑

15

Point-wise Guidelines to Face IAS Interview

It is important to follow the following strategies to do well in interview of any type and for any kind of position:

- ***First impression is the last impression:*** There exists a famous saying, 'in an interview, interviewers form their opinions about interviewee in first few minutes, rest of the time is used to reinforce those opinions'. This is due to the effect of first impression. Regarding the first impressions, a general saying is 'first impression is the last impression'. Looking at these phenomena, it is really important for you that you build good impression in the mind of the interviewers. First impression or following impressions is a matter of observation of the interviewers about you. This perception is built on the basis of totality of your personality that is revealed by you the instant you enter the interview room and your pattern of interface with the interviewers within first few minutes. They will perceive you first externally and subsequently deeply. For making good first impression on the basis of your external features, it is anticipated that your outfit should be elegant and sober, professional briefcase/portfolio/bag, professional hairstyle and other outlook. You should tread very confidently from the door to the chair in proper manner, take your seat in proper manner only after taking due permission, keep constant eye contact with the interviewer who is asking question and use proper body language. Although many of these are outward things, they express about you and are vital for constructing good first impression. For inward things, ensure that you use sweet and polite tone while talking to the interviewers or answering their questions, show your seriousness about the job and interview process even if you do not expect to join the job after being selected (in rarest of the rare case), and similar such things which show that you consider in high level of etiquette and mannerism.

- ***Be a Good Listener:*** You should be a good listener while an interview. This will assist in two-fold goals, that is, when you listen considerately, you tend to comprehend questions correctly. This will aid you to respond correctly. Second, it will help you in impressing the interviewers by generating a feeling that you are taking genuine interest in whatever they are asking about. In the whole process, your facial expression should show that you are taking active interest in what an interviewer is saying.
- ***Communicate Effectively:*** An effective communication refers to one which sends the message in a good way. In addition to sending the message effectively, effective communication also focuses on laying higher emphasis on more important matter. In written communication, this is achieved by underlining the more essential matters or putting them into italic or bold form. In oral communication, this is achieved by changing tone style backed by body language. To make your communication effective, you can work on the following points:

  Pause for some time before answering after the interviewer has finished his questions. Use apt words to complete your answer. You may use technical words for answering the questions of the same nature, but be sure to not use these technical words every time. Follow the principle of brevity. It indicates that you should answer a question in a very specific manner that is required by a question. For instance, if you have been asked to define a word, limit yourself to its definition only. Likewise, if you have been asked to narrate the features of an object, just mention the various points. Specifics of various points are not needed at this stage. If the interviewers ask for detail of any point, narrate its detail. This way, time allotted to each candidate for interviewing is utilized properly.
- ***Seek Clarification if necessary:*** If a situation arises where you fail to understand the questions properly because of lack of

appropriate loudness of voice of the interviewer, disturbance of any kind or your own inattention, do not hesitate to seek clarification for the same. Likewise, there may be chance that an interviewer may pose a question whose meaning is not as specific as wished. In such a case, you simply say, 'sir, do you mean... Do not feel afraid that the interviewer will feel agitated. In contrast, he will be happy that your method is precise, which will go in your favour. Instead of giving wrong answer to a question, it is better to ask for repetition and clarification. However, this practice, if adopted quite frequently, becomes annoying. Keep this phenomenon in your mind while using this practice.

- ***Do Not Argue with the Members:*** It is important to keep in mind that you treat an interview as a discussion forum and not an argument forum. Discussion means pondering on issues that may develop from a question. To sort out the issues, it is possible that there may be questions over questions, particularly in an in-depth interview. If an interviewer articulates his/her opinion on an issue which you do not agree with, you gently say about your reservation. If the interviewer does not agree with your view and still persists on her earlier stand, it is better not to drag this discussion to prove the interviewer wrong. If you adopt contrary practice, this will lead to negative debate and counter-argument which may go against you.
- ***Admit Your Mistake:*** Do not hesitate to accept your mistake if pointed by the interviewer. A mistake is a wrong judgment of a situation and acting on that. Therefore, committing a mistake is not very unusual phenomenon while, committing a mistake is a natural phenomenon, persisting on that mistake after it has been discovered is a gaffe. Do not bring your ego which is false in this process.
- ***Be Polite:*** It is good to maintain a polite behaviour during interview.. Even in any unpleasant situation (this may be done deliberately to test your patience), do not lose your cool. If you lose your temper to protect your ego, you may be treated as a highly emotional person. Remember that this kind of

person is not treated suitable for any job. If you are polite in the interview, it conveys that you have respect for the ideas of others; you are open-minded to accept new ideas and change your ideas which are not relevant in a given situation. If all these are done with a cool head, these will go in your favour.

- ***Display Proper Etiquette and Manner:*** Although interview is normally a formal process, sometimes it may be conducted by the interviewers in such a manner that it appears to be an informal process. This is done purposely to make a candidate uneasy so as to get maximum possible information about her/him. If such a situation comes before you, do not forget to display the etiquette and a manner of a formal interview process. It may also happen that during your interview, some refreshment is brought to the interviewers. Generally, on such an occasion, refreshment is also served to the candidate sitting in the interview room. If such a situation comes before you and the interviewers ask you to take refreshment, do not deny this offer as it is against etiquette. If you do not want to have any particular item of refreshment served (many people do not take tea or coffee at all), say politely about it and take only the remaining ones.
- ***Create Good Last Impression:*** Suppose that the interview is like a one-day cricket match: batsman gathers runs at a brisk rate during the first few overs; this rate drops in the middle overs; but this rate increases again during the last few overs to score a winning total. In the same manner, if you have created good first impression in the beginning of the interview but failed in giving the best possible answers of some questions, you can erase the memory of such failed answers by creating good last impression. For making good last impression, you can follow the same approach which you might have used in creating good first impression with a slight difference. Commonly, chairman of the interview committee closes the interview by saying to the candidate, 'thank you' and wishing him good luck.

❑❑❑

16

Significance of Knowing Some Do's and Don'ts at IAS Interview

Reach the Interview Location on Time

Being punctual is very important in life. So, try to reach at the interview location at least 15 to 20 minutes earlier than the interview schedule mentioned in the UPSC call letter. Residents of Delhi may not have much problem in reaching the interview location, which is the UPSC building known as Dhaul Pur House, located at Shahjahan road, New Delhi, as they must know this famous place. Those coming from far off places to appear for an interview should plan their journey in such a way that they reach the city sufficiently in advance. Before arriving at the interview location, make sure that you have the following items which will be required during the interview process:

- Interview call letter.
- All educational certificates, marksheets and testimonials in original as well as their photocopies.
- Your passport size photographs (3 to 4 copies).
- A folder/portfolio bag etc. to keep the above items.

After arriving at the venue of the interview, communicate with a person at the reception/UPSC gate who will let you know to whom and where you have to meet to complete the pre-interview activities.

Completing Pre-interview Activities

Like many organizations, some pre-interview formalities have to be wrapped up by every candidate in UPSC also. One has to undertake the following activities before one gets the chance to face the interview:

- Taking signatures of the candidates.
- Authentication of certificates, marksheets, testimonials, etc.
- Filing up of traveling bills or claiming traveling allowances and other permissible allowances.
- Any other activities specified therein.

After the above activities, you are required to wait in a waiting room for your turn to come. During the waiting period, be relaxed and do not think about the interview as it will create anxiety in you. You may read some literature. You may find some newspapers/ magazines in the waiting room of the UPSC or else you are advised to carry some of your own. If you wish, you can talk to other candidates as well. But do not show your eagerness in finding what the candidate before you have spoken in the interview or what questions have been asked to her/him etc. It is a fact that everyone has to face interview with unique results, so do not take tension or worry for unnecessary things. Do avoid them. If waiting period proves to be too long, do not be impatient. In fact, in many cases this waiting period, if it is too long, becomes boring. Therefore, find areas to overcome the boring and anxiety-producing phenomenon. The best way is to read the newspapers and introspect on some of the editorial analysis.

Interview Outfit

Your outfit for the interview is bound to give you headache. Many aspirants feel perplex about how they should be dressed. This phenomenon is natural as the first interview of an interviewee is quite significant for his/her career. A poor performance in the first interview is likely to demoralize him/her, while a good performance is likely to boost his/her morale. This morale is quite important for success. Interview attire is important because it reflects the total personality of a person, her way of thinking and doing, and her approach in life. Dignified attire helps in creating good first impression in the mind of the interviewers. Therefore, in deciding your interview attire, take into account your age, position for which you are to be interviewed, dress code of the organization (UPSC) concerned and season of the interview (normally it is autumn, but may change in few years). Be ensured that your attire meets the following necessities:

- Never confuse an interview with a social function. Your outfit should be as per the requirements. Do not don a vulgar outfit.
- Your outfit should be rightly tight; not too tight that you cannot sit comfortably; not too loose to be over-sized. Your attire should be neat and well ironed. It is not important that you wear only new dress. It is preferable that you wear a dress which is not shiny but sober.

Interview Attires for Women

For a woman aspirant, following guidelines will help you in deciding your interview attire:

- *Dress:* You have a choice either to wear a lady suit or a sari on the basis of your comfort level and personality. In majority of the cases, women look good in Saris, thereby making saris more preferable. In such a case, you should wear single-light coloured sari with matching blouse. Printed suit having large-sized design should be avoided. Similarly, trousers and shirt should also be avoided unless you want to make your own personality statement. Jeans are not a strict no-no.
- *Others:* Avoid jewellery to the maximum possible level. Try to keep your clothes simple, leaning towards conservative. Apply minimum make-up/cosmetics and avoid long polished nails. If you want to carry a purse, it should be small and matching with your style as you might be needed to carry a portfolio for keeping your required documents. Your hair style should match your professional wants.

Interview Attires for Men

For a male aspirant, following guidelines will help you in deciding your interview attire:

- *Dress:* You should wear a light-coloured shirt (white or light blue), a blue or steel grey trousers and a matching tie. But, you can also choose navy blue or grey colour fabric. If the fabric has stripes, these should be of very light colour; otherwise, these are likely to overshadow your personality. Full sleeves off-white, sky blue or cream colour shirt is preferable. Avoid dark striped shirts. For a tie, avoid multicolour printed shades. Your tie should match your suit. Socks should be of a dark colour, preferably navy blue or dark grey. Shoes should be of leather with laces. Colour of shoes may be black or dark brown; but, preferably use black leather shoes, which are neatly polished. Both shoes and socks should be matching each other. Your interview is going to be scheduled during Autumn, which is like summer in Delhi, so choose your shirt and trousers as mentioned above. Tie of the matching colour is preferable. Avoid half-sleeve shirt even though you may be required to wear this type of shirt at your work place. Similarly, jeans should be avoided.

- ***Others:*** In addition to dress, you may need to take care of other items of outfit. Avoid wearing rings even if you are wearing them regularly. Rings with stones should be avoided at the time of interview. Wearing a wrist watch will be enough and avoid fragrances and cologne that have high smell content. Your hair style should be of professional.

❑❑❑

17
Ways to Do Better in IAS Interview

If you get an interview, then you've vaulted from one out of 100–200 to a select group of 5–7. Now the competition is much stiffer even as the odds become far better. Some of the critical suggestions and guidelines include:

1. ***Dress code.*** A professional dress code is essential. It's expected of you as it's an interview for job. In case you feel 'that's just not me', then at least you can wear something that could be between casual and professional. It is to be noted that you'll also be meeting with a dean and probably even a provost, whose thinking about how to dress can be different from those of several faculty members. Having said that, what to wear does depend, in some instances, on where you've applied, and based on that you need to determine the dress code.
2. ***Reaching for the interview.*** First, you need to use the restroom. You need to check out your appearance. It may be a small thing, yet very crucial. I know a fellow who thinks it can cost him a job. He'd had a piece of cake and a cup of coffee before his interview. When he got there he was ushered in to meet the search committee. He thought it went fine, though he felt some unease in the room. As he left he went to the restroom and discovered, to his horror, that there was chocolate around his mouth. 'And they looked at me for an hour without saying a word. But what must they have thought?' he groaned. He didn't get the job.
3. ***Deliberating your research.*** The time to do this is during the formal interview with the committee. But be brief. Note that they will be looking to see if you're too long-winded. This may give the impression that you lack focus and are not organized. The question about your long-term interests is very significant and they're likely to ask it: 'Where do you see yourself 10

years from now?' They're looking for a possible 10- to 20-year commitment. Project that you're a straight-shooter, but don't do it to the extent where honesty becomes synonymous with abrasiveness.

4. ***Social conditions.*** At lunch time or other social opportunities, concentrate on the research your interviewers are doing rather than your own if the conversation is an academic one. If it's personal, give them some idea of your interests and background, but try to quickly shift the conversation to their lives. It exhibits interest in others and also reduces the risk that something about your personal life might turn them off. In general, understand that most people would rather talk about what they're doing, be it their work or pleasure, than what you're doing. That's about life.
5. ***Personality.*** In general, being personable is important. Of course, being intellectually qualified comes first. But then, once you've met the standard in that region, what you're like as a human being becomes important. Note that an academic job is a lifetime gig. No one wants to give tenure to a jerk. If you come across in any way as nasty, conceited, inflexible, weird, in short, 'difficult', as they say euphemistically, you're not going to be hired, no matter how smart or productive you are. Why? Because departments are terrified that they'll give someone tenure and then be stuck with a person they hate. In short, they don't want to be wrong about this decision. A sense of humour is always useful. If you don't have that, develop it. You should always aspire them to say later that they really enjoyed meeting you.
6. ***The job conversation.*** Suppose most of your audience hasn't read the articles or papers you've sent them. Therefore, you should play it really safe and discuss something that even people who are completely out of your area will comprehend. Simultaneously, you should also present some advanced stuff so that no one will say your talk was simplistic. Keep track of your time limit. By this time of the day the search committee is getting tired in general and some of them won't have the

patience to listen for very long. Using Power Point is fine. It gives people something to look at. Ensure to allow enough time for questions because that's what they'll most enjoy doing and you certainly don't want them to think you're scared of being stumped, even if you may be.

In case they're critical of what you say, don't get defensive. Accept the possible validity of their comments and then try to respond as best as you can. Never knock a person's question. Saying: 'I'm glad you asked that', or 'That's an interesting point' is a good way to respond. Note that if you in any way embarrass a questioner, you're probably finished. They'll not only be just annoyed rather they'll start lobbying against you.

Post Interview

Ensure to follow up with a nice thank-you letter describing them how much you enjoyed the day, how much you liked the department and show your interest in coming again. Do it a few days later, while their memory of who you are is still fresh. Of course they'll see it as an effort to land the position, but they still want to hear it. Think of how uninterested you'll look if you don't send a letter. If you receive an offer, don't be afraid to ask for more money, no matter how good you think the offer is. They have no idea that you think it's a great deal and you shouldn't tell them. No offer was ever rescinded, as far as I know, because someone asked for more; at that stage, you already have the job. More than likely, they'll respect you for it. Be careful with joint appointments. They can make you more attractive to the college, but you need to understand the exact deal upfront.

Ultimately, even if you don't get an offer, it's not compulsorily over. Their first choice may have a change of heart and that may result in the committee turning to you. These ideas, some of them counterintuitive, apply to most, but not all, situations. You must be ready to adapt them to the specific institution. And above all, keep in mind, that the market is very competitive. That's not surprising when you think that there are very few jobs that are guaranteed for life if you perform reasonably well at them for five or seven years.

❑❑❑

18

Importance of Developing Interview Skills among Candidates

Significance of Personality Development

There are two purposes of personality development: first is to achieve success in material life and the second is to achieve success in spiritual life. For both purposes it requires to have balanced and developed faculties like physical body with sharp sense organs and working organs, concentration, memory, sensitivity, emotions like love (concern) and enlightened ego, will power, confidence, courage, good discrimination, intelligence and many others. Power, fame and money or all the three are one set of components of life. Though they are considered harmful to human growth, these are important for getting success in material life. Man can use them for betterment of society. Simplicity, knowledge, and happiness or all the three are another set of components of life and they are important for getting success in spiritual life. These can be achieved only by development of personality. What is personality? The word personality comes from the Latin word persona which means the 'mask'. The masks were used in dramas to show different characters, emotions and behaviour. In Sanskrit 'vyaktitva' is the word for personality, which means the essence of vyakti (human being). Hence, personality means the essence of character and behaviour of an individual. It has two important dimensions: one is internal and the other is the external. Internal personality means the essence of character and behaviour of oneself with the internal world and the external personality means essence of character and behaviour of oneself with the external world. Both dimensions of personality are interconnected, inter-related and interdependent on each other.

❑❑❑

Elements and Dimensions of Personality Development

Based on guna, there are three kinds of personalities: tamasika, rajasika and sattvika. Tamasika means lethargic; this type of personality doesn't like to work; such people are hypo-active and feel inferior. They accumulate or suppress energy. Rajasika means hyper-active; this type of personality always wants some kind of action and feels superior. They spend their energy unnecessarily. Sattvika personality means to be always in a balanced state. This type of personality works hard, tirelessly and will enjoy the work while working and also feels comfortable in no-work situations. They will always conserve their energy for development of personality. The notable point is that out of these three, anyone can dominate human life and the activity of other two is lesser in degree and all these personality types work on the personality of man as a whole.

Internal Personality

Internal personality is considered to be as deep as the ocean and as expansive as the space. Scientists of the present era have been doing their research on the external world by using their external personality but all the seers in ancient India have done their research using their internal personality. The internal personality of a human being has five bodies' i.e. physical body, mental body, emotional body, intellectual body and spiritual body. All these bodies are inter-connected, inter-related and inter-dependent.

External Personality

Nobody is an island; an individual is constantly in relation with the external world and always interacts with it i.e. material world, vegetable world, animal world, human being (family, society, nation and humanity) and cosmos. Everything in this universe is an expression of Ishwara (ultimate force). Therefore, they are inter-connected, inter-related and inter-dependent on each other.

Importance of Personality Development

Personality development refers to the development of the organized pattern of behaviours and attitudes that makes a person distinctive. Personality development is the result of the on-going interaction of temperament, character, and environment.

Personality is something that makes a person unique, and it can be recognized soon after birth. A child's personality has several components: temperament, environment, and character. Temperament is the set of genetically determined traits that determine the child's approach to the world and how the child learns about the world. There are no genes that specify personality traits, but some genes do control the development of the nervous system, which in turn controls behaviour. A second component of personality comes from adaptive patterns related to a child's specific environment. Most psychologists agree that these two factors—temperament and environment—influence the development of a person's personality the most. Temperament, with its dependence on genetic factors, is occasionally denoted as 'nature', whereas the environmental factors denote 'nurture'.

Though controversy still exists as to which factor ranks higher in affecting personality development, all experts agree that high-quality parenting plays a significant role in the development of a child's personality. When parents understand how their child responds to certain situations, they can anticipate issues that might be problematic for their child. They can prepare the child for the situation or in some cases they may avoid a potentially difficult situation altogether. Parents who know how to adapt their parenting approach to the particular temperament of their child can best provide guidance and ensure the successful development of their child's personality. Finally, the third component of personality is character—the set of emotional, cognitive, and behavioural patterns learned from experience that determines how a person thinks, feels, and behaves. A person's character continues to evolve throughout life, although much depends on inborn traits and early experiences. Character also depends on a person's moral development.

In 1956, psychiatrist Erik Erikson gave an insightful description on how personality develops as per his extensive experience in psychotherapy with children and adolescents from low, upper, and middle-class backgrounds. According to Erikson, the socialization process of an individual consists of eight phases, each one accompanied by a 'psychosocial crisis' that must be solved if the person is to manage the next and subsequent phases satisfactorily. The stages significantly affect personality development, with five of them taking place during infancy, childhood, and adolescence.

❖ Infancy

During the first two years of life, an infant goes through the first stage: Learning Basic Trust or Mistrust (Hope). Well-nurtured and loved, the infant develops trust and security and a basic optimism. Badly handled, the infant becomes insecure and learns 'basic mistrust'.

❖ Toddlerhood

The second stage takes place during early childhood, between about 18 months to two years and three to four years of age. It deals with Learning Autonomy or Shame (Will). Well-parented, the child emerges from this stage with self-confidence, elated with his or her newly found control. The early part of this stage can also comprise of stormy tantrums, stubbornness, and negativism based on the child's temperament.

❖ Preschool

The third stage takes place during the 'play age', or the later preschool years from about three to entry into formal school. The developing child goes through Learning Initiative or Guilt (Purpose). The child learns to use imagination; to broaden skills through active play and fantasy; to cooperate with others; and to lead as well as to follow. If unsuccessful, the child becomes fearful, is unable to join groups, and harbours guilty feelings. The child is dependent more on adults and is restricted both in the developing play skills and imagination.

❖ School Age

The fourth stage, Learning Industry or Inferiority (Competence), takes place during school age, up to and possibly including junior high school. The child understands as how to master more formal skills:

- Relating with peers according to rules
- Progressing from free play to play that is structured by rules and requires teamwork (team sports)
- Understanding fundamental intellectual skills (reading, arithmetic)

At this stage, the need for self-discipline increases every year. The child who, because of his or her successful passage through earlier stages, is trusting, autonomous and full of initiative, will have a tendency to learn to be industrious. However, the mistrusting child will have a tendency to doubt the future and will feel inferior.

❖ Adolescence

The fifth stage, Learning Identity or Identity Diffusion (Fidelity), takes place during adolescence from age 13 or 14. Maturity starts developing during this time; the young person acquires self-certainty as opposed to self-doubt and experiments with different constructive roles rather than adopting a negative identity, such as delinquency. The well-adjusted adolescent actually looks forward to achievement, and, in later adolescence, clear sexual identity is established. The adolescent seeks leadership (someone to inspire him or her), and gradually develops a set of ideals to live by. The Child Development Institute (CDI) rightfully points out that very little knowledge is available on the type of specific environment that will result, for example, in traits of trust being more developed in a person's personality. Helping the child through the various stages of emotional and personality development is a complex and difficult task. Searching for the best ways of accomplishing this task accounts for most of the research carried out in the field of child development today. Renowned psychologist Carl Rogers emphasized how childhood experiences affect personality development. Many psychologists believe that there are certain critical periods in personality development—periods when the child will be more sensitive to certain environmental factors. Most experts believe that a child's experiences in the family are important for his or her personality development, although not exactly as described by Erikson's stages, but in good agreement with the importance of how a child's needs should to be met in the family environment. For example, children who are toilet trained too early or have their toilet training carried out too strictly may become rebellious. Another example can be shown by children who learn appropriate behaviour to their sex life when they have a good relationship with their same-sex parent.

Another environmental factor of significance is culture. Researchers comparing cultural groups for specific personality types have found some significant differences. For instance, Northern European countries and the United States have individualistic cultures that put more emphasis on individual needs and accomplishments. In contrast, Asian, African, Central American, and South American countries are characterized more by community-centred cultures that focus on belonging to a larger group, such as a family, or nation. In these cultures, cooperation is believed to be a more significant value than competitiveness, which will compulsorily affect personality development.

□□□

19

Guidelines to Enhance Interview Skills

Good skills to face an interview are of utmost importance as even the smartest and most qualified job seekers require to prepare for job interviews. Why, you ask? Being a critical step, there is only one chance to make a great first impression. So go through these 10 tactics to improve your interview skills.

- ***Rehearse Good Nonverbal Communication***

  It's about showing confidence: standing in a straight posture, making eye contact and connecting with a good, firm handshake. That first nonverbal impression can be a great beginning — or quick ending — to your interview.

- ***Dress for the Job or Company***

  It is important to dress in a formal way while going for an interview. It is good to look professional and well-groomed. Whether you don a suit or something less formal rests on the company culture and the position you are seeking. If possible, call to find out about the company dress code before the interview.

- ***Listen***

  Since the talks start regarding the interview, your interviewer is giving you information, either directly or indirectly. If you are paying heed to it, you are missing a major opportunity. Good communication skills means listening and letting the person know you heard what was said. Observe your interviewer, and match that style and pace.

- ***Don't Talk Too Much***

  You should know the limits where you need to stop conveying about yourself to the interviewer. When you have not prepared ahead of time, you may ramble when answering interview questions, sometimes talking yourself right out of the job. Rehearse for the interview by knowing the job posting, matching your skills with the position's requirements and relating only that information.

- ***Don't Be Too Familiar***

  The interview can be defined as a professional meeting to talk business. This is not a process to make a new friend. Your level of familiarity should mimic the interviewer's demeanour. It is vital to bring energy and enthusiasm to the interview and to ask questions, but do not overstep your place as a candidate looking for a job.

- ***Use Fitting Language***

  Be sure to use professional language during the interview. Avoid using any inappropriate slang words or references to age, race, religion, politics or sexual orientation as they could send you out the door very quickly.

- ***Don't Be Cocky***

  Attitude plays a key role in your interview success. There exists a fine balance between confidence, professionalism and modesty. Even if you're putting on a show to exhibit your ability, overconfidence is as bad, if not worse, as being too reserved.

- ***Take Care to Answer the Questions***

  When an interviewer seeks an example of a case when you did something, he is looking for a sample of your past behaviour. If you miss to relate a specific example, you not only do not answer the question, but you also slip a chance to prove your ability and talk about your skills.

- ***Ask Questions***

  If you fail to ask any question when you are given chance by an interviewer, consider it a wrong step. Asking questions demonstrates an interest in what goes on in the company. Asking questions also gives you the chance to find out if this is the right place for you. The best questions come from listening to what you're asked during the interview and asking for additional information.

- ***Don't Appear Anxious***

  You make your chances of getting selected grim if you interview with the 'please, please hire me' approach. It is important to maintain the three C's during the interview: cool, calm and confident. You know you can do the job; make sure the interviewer believes you can, too.

❑❑❑

20

How to Rehearse for Civil Services Interview?

The nature of Interview is slightly dissimilar from your prelims and mains examination. As your knowledge is already tested during Prelims and Mains, Interview mainly aims to assess your personality. The former exams have already established that you are very good at expression, memory, analysis and writing. Now what they want to test is your qualities as an officer. When you will become an officer, how you will take the decisions. They will observe you as future administrators, and they will make an attempt to fit you into the frame of an administrator. They want to test that how far you qualified for that framework or eligible for the post. Now the first Mantra is that Know Yourself and Present yourself, as you are. So it is fundamentally a test of your personality. The committee members will observe how you think, tackle issues and face pressures. If you observe the patterns, you will see that they like to test you in pressure situations. So, the thing is to be tested here is how you stand in pressure. Whether you lose your calm, react suddenly, try to run away or you face the reality that sorry sir I don't know. Hence, it is also a test of your understanding and how you think. So, First mantra is Know yourself and Present yourself as you are. It happens many a times that we really fail to understand ourselves and our own capabilities. So the main thing to learn is to try to know WHO I AM? And it not be as fluent in English as Shakespeare and not be as good in mathematical or analytical ability as scientist. Whatever is your ability should be presented in front of them.

There shouldn't be Any Artificiality

You need to be real if you want to be successful in the process of interview. If you try to fake your personality, there are maximum chances of getting caught. The Interview panels/boards may be different every time with various members working for the common goal, that is, to select an able candidate, you should be sure to present yourself as you are. Be confident and believe in yourself with the thinking that you deserve where you are after studying hard for more than 2 decades of your life. Now, whatever the size or style of the board, they will judge you whether you are fit for this job or not. So, do not indulge in artificial drama. So, your presence of mind and how instant you answer is actually expression of yourself. Generally, few question they will ask from your education, background or place somewhere you come from. Few question from current affairs, about subject you opted for civil services or civil services in general, about challenges that India faces in general. There is always difference of opinions as there exist many answers to open-ended questions. There is no right answer to certain issues, they are still debated and still going on. The following should be kept in mind:

Point is: Every answer which has sound reasoning, and I should be able to justify my answer.

(While explaining/answering)

I should not say that: 'This should be done because, I feel so'.

I should be saying: 'This should be done because I think so'.

Therefore, you should be able to think and justify your answer in a fair manner.

There always exist inconsistency and contradiction in thought process of those who read some newspaper and information sources and then just reproduce that in interview or exam. It reflects lack of self-analysis. One must have a consistent way of analysing happenings and way of looking at things, and only then your answer will be different because that will be your own answer.

❑❑❑

21

Tips to Prepare for Proper Answers to Questions during Interview

Preparation is a Must before the Interview

1. ***Two types of questions can be asked.*** First specific question about the job is to see if you have the skills to do the job. Second 'Human Resource' questions that are designed to see if you have the right personality to fit in the team. Being good at both types of questions to be able to get the job is important.
2. ***Some 'Human Resource' questions include:*** How do you work in a team? Can you work alone? (I work well in a team and I can work alone when I have to). Where do you see yourself ten years from now? (I see myself doing the same job and maybe moving up a little in position and becoming more 'Senior'). Why are you changing jobs? (I have learned a lot in my current position and I would like to work for a firm with more challenge and more responsibility). What salary are you looking for? (If you mention an amount it looks bad unless you are grossly underpaid. I say, 'I am open'). What don't you like about your current position? (Don't mention anything bad, say, 'I am happy with my current position, the benefits and the pay, I was told about this position and on the 'spur of the moment' decided to go in an interview). Tell me your weaknesses (If you are honest, they will not hire you. Rather tell them that you do not like when you are asked to figure out who to lay-off or that the drive is too long).
3. Practice well in advance by studying your resume, make it as clear and provocative as you can. Look through it for any add-ons or tweaks that you would like to fit in before you will be put to hand it in. Read through it a few times so you are familiar with what your resume reads off. Look for a family member

or friend who could read it out loudly so they can spot errors, instead of interviewer pin-point your mistake.

4. Practice answering some questions by playing the interviewer game! All you need is at least 4 friends or family members and a list of different interview questions (at least 5 questions per person). Have your friend/family members ask you questions, each using their own way of expressing it to you. They will enjoy it, so will you, and in turn you get the practice for your interview!
5. Do this interview every day for a week so that you could get the experience of being interviewed. This simple exercise assists your nerves calm down as you have a better understanding of what to expect, and you could feel polished up and ready for the big day of interview.
6. Go for shopping the day before your interview. Now, you don't need to spend loads of money, but you need to look presentable. Women: A simple black or grey pantsuit with an elegant blouse under topped off with a stylish sweater and heels. Men: Go with a suit. No need for the tux to come out from behind the closet, but the pants sure can. Use an elegant shirt and some dressy shoes. Your hair, and yourself, should smell good. Do you get nervous the day before? Grandma's tip: Get about a cup of 2% milk and pour it in a cooking pan. Set your stove on medium and let it stir for about 2 minutes, or until it's warm. Put in some powdered chocolate and add about 2-3 tiny marshmallows. The milk helps to cool down your nerves while you eat a sweet treat. You should also get your rest. Go to bed at approximately 9:30 so you will be well rested. Remember to wear perfume/cologne to smell good. Your appearance counts, sometimes as much as your smarts. If you feel good, it is likely that you perform better during the interviews.

Steps to be followed at the Interview

1. Calm down, and always think yourself that you have come prepared and that you look great. Before entering the interview room, make sure that you are relaxed, comfortable, confident,

and, definitely, focused. Drink about an inch tall of ice cold water to let something go through yourself before the interview. Make sure you don't drink more than needed and you get a potty break right before the 'view. Put some chap stick for dry, cracked, peeled lips but smile.

2. Wait! Before you walk in there, ensure that your phone is OFF, even a vibrating phone attracts attention where it's not needed (or wanted). Ensure everything is ready and set for your 'view. Your entrance is vital, also, so walk in with poise: put up your smile and confidence before walking for the interview.
3. When a hard question arises, be able to analyse the questions in your mind. Accept the difficulty. Repeat over something such as: 'That was a difficult question. However, I would like to provide you with an accurate answer, so I will have to think about that for a minute'. Let off a small smile at the end and go back to searching: Take your time, but don't take hours to answer the simplest question. And do not repeat over again and again through simple questions. You need to take time for everything.
4. Honesty applies good for all, particularly when part of the test is on honesty/loyalty. Calm down and take time to answer questions honestly, but let the metaphoric light shine on you in a good way. You need to answer questions with honesty, poise, smiles, pauses, and you might just be on your way back there tomorrow!
5. Think about different types of questions, tricky or otherwise. Ensure you are giving your body sufficient time to analyse all the questions. Think about them and never let one slide. Before you say something stupid, think about it twice if this would ruin or revive your reputation.
6. Learn to pick the best answer. Let's say, for argument's sake, that the interviewer asks, 'Why should we give you this employment opportunity, out of curiosity?' You know you have about three answers to that. Answer Choice One: because I need food to eat and shelter above my dang head! Answer

Choice Two: Because this is what I love to do. Answer Choice Three: You and your company should give me this opportunity (noticed how I rephrased the question?) because I can bring in new ideas to this company. I have the creativity and thoughts about making my job easier, neater, and, overall, smarter which benefits this company. You should also give me this opportunity because I deserve to be here and have had over [state the years; months] of training/experience. The best answer is irrevocably Answer Choice Three.

7. Always put a smile during your interview, not weird, but a relaxed homey smile. Do not let your interview shake you, it's part of the whole interview thing, it's a test! Keep your cool and answer thoroughly, try your best. Do not boast because you have practiced, there's never anything like the real thing. Put up a professional, humble, and yourself attitude.

Methods to Tackle Interview Properly

The interview is one of the most vital components in the process of job search. When an employer invites you to an interview, he/she is indicating an interest in bringing you on board. The interview gives both of you the opportunity to exchange enough information to determine if you are a good 'fit' for each other. Think of an interview as a highly focused professional conversation. You should use the limited amount of time you have to learn about an employer's needs and discuss the ways you can meet these needs. In many cases, you will interview at least twice before being hired for a position. Once in a brief screening interview and at least once again in a more serious meeting when you may also speak with many of your potential coworkers. The job interview is a strategic conversation with a purpose. Your goal is to show the employer that you have the skills, background, and ability to do the job and that you can successfully fit into the organization and its culture. The interview is also your opportunity to gather information about the job, the organization, and future career opportunities to figure out if the position and work environment are right for you. Most employers do not hire people based on merit alone. Personality, confidence, enthusiasm, a positive outlook, and excellent interpersonal and communication skills count heavily in the selection process. After your cover letter and résumé, the interview is your best opportunity to wow the employer-regardless of your background and experience. To do this, use every possible strategy to develop effective interviewing skills. The best way is to prepare a selective presentation of your background, thoughtful answers to potential interview questions, well-researched questions about the organization, and an effective strategy to market yourself. Also consider your career goals and what the available job offers so that you can discuss both of these topics with employers. Interviewing is a skill that improves and becomes easier with practice. Try finding out with your school career centre or your local Employment Service office to see if it offers workshops and individual videotaped mock interviews for practice.

- ***Research:*** It is good for your advantage only that you carefully research the job and the organization. There are many ways to do this. You can request printed materials from the employer, such as annual reports and job descriptions. This is an entirely appropriate request, so don't hesitate to make it. Use your library and career centre resources. Ask colleagues, friends, and faculty about the organization, and about any personal contacts at the organization they might have. Look at the organization's home page. Understanding the job will help you prepare a list of your qualifications such that you can show point by point, why you are the best candidate.
- ***Practice is Crucial:*** Design a succinct, clear answer to each of the questions in the interview questions section. Practice answering questions with a friend, or in front of a mirror. Ask your friend to give you constructive criticism on your speaking style, mannerisms, and poise. As you practice, avoid colloquialisms, such as 'like' and 'you know'. Make sure you don't script all your answers-you'll sound as though you're reading cue cards! It's significant that you prepare yourself for talking with complete strangers.

- ***Understand the Logistics of the Interview:*** The more you understand, the more focused you can be while answering. Find out when the interview is scheduled, what to expect during it, and how long you will be there. Also look for if you will be talking to just one person or to more than one.
- ***Be Active and Professional:*** Always arrive early. If you don't know where the organization is located, call for exact directions in advance. Leave some extra time for any traffic, parking, or unpredictable events. If you are running late, call right away and let someone know. The best time to arrive is approximately 5–10 minutes early. Give yourself the time to read your résumé one more time, to catch your breath, and to be ready for the interview. Once you're at the office, treat everyone you encounter with respect. Present your pleasing personality to everyone as soon as you walk in for the interview.
- ***Proper Dress for Your Success:*** Wear a professional business suit. This point cannot be emphasized enough. First impressions are extremely important in the interview process. Women should avoid wearing too much jewellery or make up. Men should avoid flashy suits or wearing too much cologne. It is also important that you feel comfortable. While a suit is the standard interview attire in a business environment, if you think it is an informal environment, call before and ask. Regardless, you can never be overdressed if you are wearing a tailored suit.
- ***Always Be Organized:*** Always keep a portfolio notepad or at the very least a manila file folder labelled with the employer's name. Bring extra résumés and have the names, addresses and phone numbers of references, in case the employer asks. Also, bring a list of questions for the employer. You may refer to your list of questions to be sure you've gathered the information you need to make a decision. Never be preoccupied with taking down notes during the interview.
- ***Understand Yourself:*** You can make the interview process easier for the employer if you volunteer relevant information about yourself. Think how you would like to present your strengths, experiences, education, work style, skills and goals.

Be prepared to supplement all your answers with examples that support the statements you make. It is also a good idea to review your résumé with a critical eye and identify areas that an employer might see as limitations or want further information. Think how you can answer difficult questions with accuracy and positivity, while keeping each answer brief.

- ***Be Honest:*** An interview presents the employer an opportunity to get to know you. When you want to market yourself to the employer, put forth the answer ready for each question with an honest response.
- ***Be Positive:*** Do not tell anything negative about past experiences, employers or courses and professors. Always think of something positive about an experience and talk about that. You should also keep up your enthusiasm. If you are really interested in the job, try informing the interviewer with all honesty.
- ***Put forth Your Interest:*** One of the best methods to show you are interested in a job is to demonstrate that you have researched the organization before the interview. You can also show interest by asking questions about the job, the organization, and its services and products. The best way to impress an employer is to ask questions that build upon your interview discussion. This shows you are interested and paying close attention to the interviewer. It is a good idea to prepare a few questions in advance, but an insightful comment based on your conversation can make an even stronger statement. At the end of an interview, it is always right for you to ask when you may expect to hear from the employer.
- ***Keep the Salary Discussion for Later:*** Find out as much as you can before the interview about the levels of salary for the position you are looking for. Do not come up with the issue of salary at the time of the first interview. If the interviewer asks about your salary expectations, give only a general answer, such as that your expectations appears to be close to their range.
- ***Notes Post-Interview:*** Post-interview, be smart enough to take time to write down the names and titles (check spelling) of

all your interviewers, your impressions, remaining questions and any information that may affect your decision to accept a position with the organization. If you are taking up interviews on a regular basis, this will help you keep employers and circumstances clearly differentiated.

- ***Follow Up Is Always Important:*** You should pen down a thank you note within 48 hours post-interview, even if the interview (or the interviewer) was not productive and/or you are not interested in the position. It is important to say thank you for the time the interviewer spared for you. This letter should be written in short. (Refer to the section on writing thank you letters.)

❑❑❑

22

Significance of Knowing the Structure of Interview

Before you receive a job offer from an employer, you will typically have a number of interviews. The first interview is a screening interview that is conducted either over the phone or at the employer's office. On-campus interviews are regarded as the screening interviews. Screening interviews are brief, generally lasting for 30 to 60 minutes. During that time, the employer will want you to elaborate on experiences and skills outlined in your résumé. Many employers use the screening interview as a chance to describe the organization and the position. If the employer is impressed with your performance in this interview, you will be invited to a second (and perhaps third or fourth) interview. The second interview is longer, lasting anywhere from two hours to a whole day. It could include a variety of questions, some form of testing, lunch or dinner, a tour, as well as a series of interviews with various employees. You should get a thorough understanding of the organization's culture and environment, job responsibilities and other related information to decide on a job offer if extended after the end of the second round of interview.

- ***Warm-Up:*** Each interview rather has a predictable pattern of warm-up, information exchange, and wrap-up conversations. During the initial few moments of the interview (the warm-up), an employer will be formulating a first, lasting impression of you. The way you greet the employer, the firmness of your handshake, and the way you are dressed, will all be a part of this initial impression. An interviewer may begin by asking common-ground questions about shared interests, the weather, or your travel to the interview. Some interviewers might start by saying 'Tell me about yourself'. This is an opportunity for you to briefly discuss your background, skills, and interest in the position.

- ***Exchange of the Information:*** The exchange of information will be the mainly part of the interview. This is when you will be asked the most questions and learn the most about the employer. In screening interviews, many employers will spend more time describing their opportunities than asking you specific questions. The reverse will be true in second interviews. Interview questions may range from 'Why did you choose to pursue a business degree?' to 'What are your strengths/weaknesses?' and 'What are your long-range career goals?' If you are prepared for the interview, you will be able to emphasize your qualifications effectively as you respond to each question. By practicing for interviews, you will boost your confidence and will be in a position to put forth more polished answers during future interviews.
- ***The Wrap-up:*** Finally, it's likely that the employer will ask, 'Do you have any questions?' This is the clue that the interview is going to end very soon. Do ask questions. This will demonstrate your research and interest in the job. Your questions might be direct, logistical questions such as, 'When can I expect to hear from you?' (if that has not been discussed); questions to clarify information the employer has presented; a question regarding the employer's use of new technology or practices related to the career field; or a question to assess the culture and direction of the organization such as 'Where is this organization headed in the next five years?' or 'Why do you like working for this organization?' Do not ask specific questions about salary or benefits unless the employer broaches the subject first. The employer may also ask you if you have anything else you would like to add or say. Again, it's best to have a response. You can use this opportunity to thank the employer for the interview, summarize your qualifications, and reiterate your interest in the position. If you want to add information or emphasize a point made earlier, you can do that, too. This last impression is equally as crucial as the first impression and will certainly add to the substance discussed as part of the information exchange.

❑❑❑

23

How to Communicate Effectively in Interview?

As an interview is a two-way communication process, if you become successful in communicating your skills, experiences and interests in a proper manner, there is a good chance the employer will remember you. So it is important to keep the following rules in mind:

- ***Be yourself.*** You should show the real you. Do not try to fake your personality. Be professional, but don't be scared to let your personality shine through.
- ***Listen sensibly.*** Being careful and attentive is very important for being successful in any process.
- ***Be positive.*** Employers do not like to hear excuses or bad feelings about a negative experience. If you are asked about any negative aspect or a weakness in your background, don't be defensive. Focus instead on briefly stating the facts and what you learned from the experience.
- ***Be poised.*** It is important to pay heed to your nonverbal behaviour. Make an eye contact with the interviewer, sit up straight, control nervous habits, don't giggle or play with your hair, and smile as you are greeted.
- ***Don't be afraid of short pauses.*** It is common or good to take a short pause before starting to answer. You may need a few seconds to formulate an answer. In the same way, the interviewer may need time to form an appropriate question. It is not necessary to fill up every second with conversation.
- ***Most interviewers are seeking specific skills.*** The list of skills given as under is important to keep in mind practicing your answers and also during the interview. Employers are looking for:

- *Communication skills*. The ability to think, formulate ideas and relate them in a succinct manner.
- Leadership skills, managing, and directing people.
- Management of resources.
- Direction setting.
- Computer savvy.
- Knowledge of business and organizational management.
- Teamwork experience.
- Trustworthiness, responsibility, dependability.
- Diligence.
- Adaptability.

❑❑❑

24

Interview Practice Makes one Perfect

As saying goes, practice makes the man perfect, you also have to learn the technique and then practice, practice, practice. A mock interview will not only aid you perfect your technique, but it will also permit you to get valuable feedback and coaching on your performance. Sue is an able tennis player who has worked on her stroke and technique for many years. She has learned from her failures and success. She is now graduating from college and has applied for some on-campus interviews with recruiters. She is confident that she understands her subject and is a pretty good speaker but decides that suggestion from a professional would be a good idea. Working with a professional and getting feedback on your performance in a mock interview is similar to working with a sports coach to learn how to improve your game. Both will enable you to learn where your strengths lie and where you may need work to improve your performance. The time and effort you have put in practicing will help you greatly in either situation. Practice helps you in gaining self-confidence. In today's competitive world, you are required to be always ready to do anything. So before Sue's interviews with potential employers, she signs up for a mock interview at the campus career centre. She is provided the interview tip sheet to read before the scheduled mock interview. The tip sheet includes the following:

Mock Interview

- A 30-minute recorded session of you in an interview with a professional.
- A review of the tape with productive feedback on your presentation.

Preparation

- Arrange for the session by investigating your company/industry of interest.
- Inspect and recognize the most common industry traits desired (analytical skills, communication skills, business knowledge and problem solving).
- Frame answers to show your experience with these factors as well as responses to behavioural interview questions, such as 'Tell me about a time when...' and 'Can you give me an example of a time...'

The Session

- Don an appropriate outfit — as though this is a real company interview.
- Pay due respect to the interviewer with an enthusiastic handshake and smile.
- Pay attention to the questions put up. Understand what the interviewer wants to know from you. Ask for clarification if the question is not clear.
- Try to keep your answers short and crisp — two to three minutes long.
- Make sure you are selling the product: You.
- Should have questions framed to ask the interviewer.

The Feedback

- Notice your feelings while reviewing the tape and listening to your answers. Do you think you have communicated what you intended?
- Attend to feedback with an open mind, not defensively.
- Learn from your presentation. How are you being observed through the eyes of someone unknown?

Model Interview Replies

While giving a complex job interview, you'll be showered with many interview questions. But do you really comprehend what the interviewer wants to ask?

'Most [candidates] have no idea why a recruiter asks a particular question', says Brad Karsh, an ex-recruiter for advertising giant Leo Burnett and present president of career consulting firm Job Bound. 'They tend to think it's a competition to outwit the interviewer'. The truth is that owners have neither the time nor inclination to play games with you, particularly during hiring. Your recruiter is not attempting to outguess you, he is trying to assess your answers to six key questions:

❖ Do You Acquire the Qualities to Do the Job?

Karsh states that the recruiter must first decide whether you have the required hard talents for the position, e.g., the programming knowledge for a database administration job or the writing chops to be a newspaper reporter. 'By really probing into what the candidate has done in the past, an interviewer can tap into hard skills'. However, the recruiter is also seeking important soft skills you'll require to be successful in the job and organization, such as the quality to work well on teams or 'the requisite common sense to figure things out with some basic training', says Terese Corey Blanck, director of student development at internship company Student Experience and a partner in College to Career, a consulting firm.

❖ Do You Fit?

'Every organization's first thought is about fit and potentially fit in a certain department', says Corey Blanck. It means that the recruiter is trying to recognize not only whether you match up well with both the company's and department's actions but also whether you'll match the talents of your potential colleagues.

❖ Do You Recognize the Company and Its Purpose?

If the company fits well with your career ambitions, you'll certainly be inspired to do good work there — and stay more than a month or two, Corey Blanck reasons. 'I don't want someone to take the position because it's a job and it fits their skills', she says. 'I want them to be excited about our mission and what we do'.

❖ How Do You Stack Up Against the Competition?

You're being assessed in comparison to other aspirants for the job. In other words, this test is graded on a curve. So the recruiter will continuously be assessing your performance in comparison to other candidates'.

❖ Do You Have the Right Attitude for the Job and Firm?

'I'm always looking for someone who has a can-do type of attitude', Corey Blanck explains. 'I want someone who wants to be challenged and is internally motivated to do well'.

Blanck also states that a recruiter can't train employee regarding this important trait. 'But you can hire for it', she says. 'And if you don't, you'll end up with a lower-performing employee'.

❖ Do You need the Job?

Most recruiters recognize better than to believe everyone they interview actually needs the position being offered. They comprehend some aspirants are exploring their options, whereas others are using an interview with a company they don't care about to improve their interview abilities. Hence, you need to prove you really want the job, says Al Pollard, senior college recruiter for Countrywide Financial. 'I use the ditch-digger analogy', he says. 'Many of us can dig ditches, but few are willing to — and even fewer want to'. ❑❑❑

25

Ways/Tactics to Handle a Panel Interview

You sit alone in front of the room, waiting for the assembled strangers to bombard you with interview questions. It's really not quite that bad. In fact, there is an upside to panel interviews. You'd probably have to interact to each of these people individually at some point or the other during the whole process — this way you can get over this all at once.

Panel — or board — interviews are often known by a standard set of questions for all applicants. Typically formal and organized, this interview format is usually used in academia and government or for high-level executives. Sometimes, you'll come across a panel interview for other positions in an organization.

Preparation of Interview

Analyse beforehand what type of interview you can face. The recruiter setting up your job interview can probably give you an idea ahead of time. If you have the chance, ask how long the interview will be and who will be on the panel? You can better tailor your answers when you understand the interview conditions. And note — no matter how uncomfortable the interview situation — you are there as a professional to understand just as much about them as they are to know about you.

Multiple Perspectives, Same Purpose

How do you tackle so many interviewers in one session? The best way is to interact with them one at a time. The board or panel is not one entity, but several individuals coming together with the common goal of hiring the best candidate for the job. At the same time, each person has his own agenda or department's interest at heart. For example, the HR manager will be checking to make sure you are a good fit with the culture and people working at the company. The hiring manager will want to know about your technical skills or business know-how. And the person from accounting would like to understand if you are savvy enough to operate a business budget.

What You Can Expect from the Panel

You may be asked to throw light about instances when you exhibited particular behaviours or skill that is important to performing your desired job. This type of interviewing, known as a behavioural interview, relies on the premise that past performance is the best indicator of future behaviour. Always be prepared to provide a sort of elevator pitch — a brief summary of who you are and your career goals. This message can include your overall mission, top-level skills and interests, but not a recitation of your life's history. Be ready to share your concise message at the beginning or end of the interview. Practicing for the interview with a video or audio recorder is extremely helpful. The best interview answers include examples that are compelling, on-target and spoken with interest and some enthusiasm. When speaking, don't hesitate to lean forward. Check your posture at a table and lean forward to demonstrate interest in the position. Always be ready to look at each person who asks the question, and accordingly shift your eye contact to the other members of the interviewing team.

At the end, ensure that you get each person's business card, hopefully at the start of the interview so that you could address each person by name and later send individual thank-you notes.

Team Interviews

Other multiple-type interview is the team or 'good cop/bad cop' interview. The team generally comprises of two interviewers, one who asks the questions and one who takes notes. The two typically trade roles, which can be confusing if they have different styles. Keep in mind that these inquisitors are working together toward the same end, so treat them equally. Although these interviews can be stressful, interview practice and preparation can pay off. When you practice your answers and watch your physical presentation well in advance before the interview, you will feel more confident irrespective of the fact how many people you have to face.

❑❑❑

26

Questions That You Can Expect at the IAS Interview

- ***About Qualifications of the Candidate***
  - ❖ Talk about yourself.
  - ❖ How do you think a friend or someone who knows you well would describe your personality?
  - ❖ What do you think is your biggest weakness?
  - ❖ How can you contribute to our organization?
  - ❖ Kindly describe about your greatest professional assignment you've ever tackle successfully.
  - ❖ What accomplishment has given you a maximum sense of satisfaction?
  - ❖ Tell something about your experiences during school days.
  - ❖ What has been your most rewarding experience during college days?
  - ❖ Tell about your most important work experience.
  - ❖ How would others who have worked with you describe you?
  - ❖ Why do you think that you are the best candidate for this position?
  - ❖ Have you ever supervised any person?
- ***About Your Capability to Work in the Environment***
  - ❖ Why are you interested in this job?
  - ❖ What do you know about our organization?
  - ❖ What kind of work environment makes you feel most comfortable?
  - ❖ What are the criteria you use to analyse the organization for which you hope to work?
  - ❖ Are you a team player?
  - ❖ How do you handle work pressure?

- How do you tackle conflict while working?
- What major problem have you come across and how have you dealt with it?
- How do you rate your competitiveness?
- What do you expect from your supervisor?
- What are the qualities a successful manager should possess?
- Discuss the relationship that should be between a supervisor and those reporting to him or her.

- ***About the Career of Candidate and Personal Choices***
  - What are your long-term professional goals? When and why did you set these goals and how are you preparing yourself to achieve them?
  - What are the most important rewards you expect in your business career?
  - What do you spend your spare time?
  - What is your expectation in terms of salary?

- ***Questions Relating to Real World Situation***
  - For the most recent graduates, some difficult questions specifically tailored to discover your business potential are as follows.
    - Why did you choose [school]?
    - What led you to major in________?
    - What course have you liked the least and the most?
    - I'd be eager to know about some things that you learned in school that could be used for the desired job.
    - Do you think your grades correctly represent your abilities?
    - If you could do so, how would you plan your academic study differently? Why?
    - We have tried to hire people from your school/your major before, and they never seem to work out. What qualities put you different from them?
    - Have you ever had problems getting along with others?
    - What problems do you see in your school? How would you go about correcting them?

- ❑ What have you done that shows initiative and eagerness to work?

- ***Some Probable Hard Questions***
  - ❖ Did you ever have a group leader or boss whom you disliked? Why did you develop such dislike?
  - ❖ How would someone who dislikes you describe you?
  - ❖ Discuss a group situation in which there were difficulties. How did you tackle the situation and what was the result? What role did you play in the group? How could the group improve its performance?
  - ❖ Tell me about a time when you experienced a failure and how did you react to this situation.
  - ❖ Tell me about a time when you were under lots of pressure to meet one or more goals.
  - ❖ Tell a situation where you had to resolve a problem at work and describe how did you resolve it.
  - ❖ Give me an instance of how you are a risk taker.
  - ❖ If you could have any job in the world, what would it be?
  - ❖ What keeps you motivated?
  - ❖ Why do you want to work for us and not for our competitors?
  - ❖ Why should we hire you over everyone else we spoke to today?
  - ❖ What do you think is the most important/difficult ethical dilemma facing corporations in present day world?
  - ❖ Give a one sentence positioning statement of yourself.
  - ❖ How do you go about deciding what to do first when given a project?
  - ❖ Discuss me about an experience you have had in a working environment (school, work, or community).
  - ❖ Tell a situation where you did not agree with something your boss asked you to do and what did you do to resolve the problem.
  - ❖ Do you think you can work under pressure?
  - ❖ What did you like/dislike about your previous job?
  - ❖ Where you would like to see yourself five years from now?

- ***Questions to be Prepared for at a Stress Interview***
  - ❖ Would you like to take the position of your boss?
  - ❖ Look at this pen I'm holding? Sell it to me.
  - ❖ Why should I hire an outsider when I could fill the job with someone from within the organization?
  - ❖ Why were you out of work for so long?
  - ❖ Tell a situation when your work or an idea was criticized.
  - ❖ Your application shows you have been with one organization for a long time without any significant increase in rank or salary. Could you tell something about this?
- ***Questions to be Prepared for by Career Changers***
  - ❖ Why would you be eager in this kind of work?
  - ❖ How do you expect to get up to speed in all the areas which will not be familiar to you?
- ***Most Commonly Asked Question, 'Tell Us about Yourself'***
  - ❖ This is also your amazing opportunity. You are likely to be asked this, so plan to use the open-ended nature of the question to your advantage. It is not necessary to answer autobiographically. You may make a choice to organize your thoughts around your interest in the job and why you are ready to do it.

❑❑❑

27

Frequently Asked Potential Questions during Interview

Since there are as many different possible interview questions as there are interviewers, you always need to be ready for anything. So we've prepared a list of 100 potential interview questions. Will you face them all? We pray no interviewer would be that cruel. Will you face a few? Probably. Will it be of any benefit even if you're not asked these exact questions? Absolutely.

Fundamental Questions during Interview

- Tell me about yourself.
- What are your strengths?
- What are your weaknesses?
- Why do you want this job?
- Where would you like to be in your career five years from now?
- What's your ideal company?
- What attracted you to this company?
- Why should we hire you?
- What did you like least about your last job?
- When were you most satisfied in your job?
- What can you do for us that other candidates can't?
- What were your duties while holding your last position?
- Why are you leaving your present job?
- What do you know about this industry?
- Do you know anything about our company?
- Are you ready to relocate?
- Do you want to ask any questions to me?

Interview Questions Associated with Behaviour

- What was the last project you headed and what was its results?
- Tell me an instance of a time when you felt you went above and beyond the call of duty at work.
- Can you tell an instance when your work was criticized?
- Have you ever been in a team where someone was not pulling their own weight? How did you tackle it?
- Describe an instance when you had to give someone difficult feedback. How did you tackle it?
- What is your greatest failure, and what did you learn from it?
- What irritates you about other people, and how do you tackle it?
- If I were your supervisor and asked you to do something that you disagreed with, what would be your take then?
- What was the most difficult period in your life, and how did you handle it?
- Give me an instance when you did something wrong. How did you tackle it?
- What irritates you about other people, and how do you handle it?
- Describe about a time where you had to handle conflict on the job.
- If you were at a business lunch and you ordered a rare steak and they brought it to you well done, what would you do?
- If you found out your company was doing something illegal, like fraud, what would be your take then?
- What assignment was too tough for you, and how did you manage this?
- What's the toughest decision you've taken in the last two years and how did you arrive to that decision?

- Explain how you would tackle a situation if you were required to perform multiple tasks by the end of the day, and there was no conceivable way that you could finish them.

Questions Related to Salary

- What is your salary expectation?
- What has been your salary history?
- Suppose I were to give you this salary you demanded but let you write your job description for the next year, what would it be like?

Questions Related to Career Development

- What are you looking for in terms of career development?
- How do you want to improve yourself in the next year?
- What kind of goals would you have in mind if you got this job?
- If I were to ask your last supervisor to provide you additional training or exposure, what would she suggest?

Getting Started with Questions

- How would you go about establishing your credibility as quickly as possible with the team?
- How much time will you require to make a significant contribution?
- What is your plan within the first 30 days of this job?
- If hired for this position, can you explain your strategy for the first 90 days?

More Focus on the Candidate

- How would you describe and rate your work style?
- What do you think an ideal working environment would be like?
- What do you look for so far as culture is concerned — structured or entrepreneurial?

- Tell some instances when you had some ideas or got those ideas implemented.
- What methods and tools do you utilize to keep yourself organized?
- If you had to choose one, would you consider yourself a big-picture person or a detail-oriented person?
- Tell me about your proudest achievement.
- Who was your favourite manager and why?
- What is your opinion about your previous boss?
- Was there a person in your career who really brought significant change to your life?
- What kind of person do you work best with and why?
- What are you most proud of?
- What do you like to do?
- What are your lifelong dreams?
- What do you ultimately want to become?
- What is your personal mission statement?
- What are three positive things your last boss would say about you?
- What negative thing would your last boss say about you?
- What three character traits would your friends use to describe you?
- What are three positive traits that you don't possess?
- If you were interviewing someone for this position, what traits would you look for?
- List five words that depict your character.
- Who has influenced you most in your career and how?
- What is your greatest fear?
- What is your biggest regret and why?
- What's the most important thing you learnt in school?

- Why did you choose your major?
- What will you miss about your present/last job?
- What is your greatest achievement outside of work?
- What are the qualities of a good leader? A bad leader?
- Do you think, a leader should be feared or liked?
- How do you feel about taking no for an answer?
- How would you feel about working for someone who knows less than you?
- How do you think I rate as an interviewer?
- Tell me one thing about yourself you wouldn't want me to know.
- Could you please tell me the difference between good and exceptional?
- What type of car do you drive?
- There's no right or wrong answer, but if you could be anywhere in the world right now, where would you be?
- What's the last book you read?
- What magazines do you subscribe to?
- What's the best movie you've seen in the last year?
- What would you do if you won the lottery?
- Who are your heroes?
- What do you like to do for fun?
- What do you do in your spare time?
- What is your favourite memory from childhood?

Brainteaser Questions

- How many times do a clock's hands overlap in a day?
- How would you weigh a plane without scales?
- Tell me 10 ways of using a pencil other than writing.
- Sell me this pencil.

- If you were an animal, which one would you want to be?
- Why is there fuzz on a tennis ball?
- If you could choose one superhero power, what would it be and why?
- If you could get rid of any one of the US states, which one would you get rid of and why?
- Keeping your eyes closed, describe me step-by-step method to tie my shoes. ❑❑❑

28

Vital Clues for UPSC Interview

Understanding the UPSC requirements is very crucial for success in the interview. Just like prelims and mains, understanding the requirements as prescribed by the UPSC should be the first step. Though aspirants keenly follow the Preliminary and Main exam syllabus, the requirements of UPSC with regarding interview test is missed by even serious aspirants.

It is to be noted What's given in the UPSC CSE syllabus about UPSC CSE interview? The six main points that can bring wonders for you in the IAS interview are given below. This is the most appropriate explanation in relation to IAS Interview or Personality test, based on UPSC notification for Civil Service Exam.

1. ***Questions will be on topics of general interest:*** A Board will take the interview of the candidate who will have before them a record of his/her career. He/she will be asked questions related to topics of general interest.
2. ***The purpose of the questions: To judge the mental ability of a candidate:*** The purpose of the interview is to evaluate the personal suitability of the candidate for a career in public service by a Board of competent and unbiased observers. The test aims to evaluate the mental calibre of a candidate.
3. ***These are the qualities which are evaluated:*** In broad terms, this is really an evaluation of not only his/her intellectual qualities but also social traits and his/her interest in current affairs. Some of the qualities to be evaluated are:
   - alertness of mind,
   - critical ability to assimilate,
   - clear and logical exposition,
   - the balance of assessment,
   - variety and depth of interest,

- capability for social cohesion and leadership,
- integrity associated with intellect and morality.

4. ***What is the method used in the UPSC CSE interview?***

   The method of the interview is not that of a strict cross-examination but of a natural, though directed and purposive conversation which aims to reveal the mental qualities of the candidate.

5. ***Not an evaluation of specialized knowledge; not an evaluation of general knowledge either!***

   The personality test aims not to be a test either of the specialized or general knowledge of the candidates which has already been evaluated by means of their written tests.

6. ***UPSC is searching for 'well-educated youth'!***

   It is expected that the candidates have taken an intelligent interest not only in their special subjects of academic study but also in the events which are taking place around them both within and outside their own state or country as well as in modern currents of thought and in new discoveries which could arouse the curiosity of well-educated youth.

❑❑❑

29

Importance of Having the Right Attitude in UPSC's IAS Interview

'People may hear your words, but they feel your attitude'.

– John C Maxwell

What do you mean by attitude?

Attitude is how you evaluate people, objects, events as well as ideas in your life. You can either be positive or negative about them based on your attitude. The three components in your attitude are as follows:

- The emotional component
- The cognitive component
- The behavioural component

The emotional component depends on your emotions while the cognitive component depends on your thoughts and beliefs. The behavioural component is what affects our behaviour. It can either be explicit or implicit. Explicit attitude is where you are constantly aware of your thoughts and actions whereas implicit attitude is unconscious but it still affects the behaviour. Attitude is formed over the years by our experiences and observations. Even a simple advertisement has the ability to alter your thought patterns and hence affect your attitude.

This type of attitude building is referred to as 'classical conditioning'. The other type of conditioning called as 'Operant Conditioning' develops from other people's thinking. An instance of this kind of conditioning is kids trying to be like their parents.

Attitude affects your behaviour and can be changed. It can be changed in two ways, by either getting influenced or motivated. An individual with a positive attitude is a thousand times more likely to succeed than an individual with a negative mind-set. Your attitude affects both you as a person as well as the people around you.

The world does not recognize you for your talent and success as much as it does for your attitude. Success or failure in life is not always a result of your hard work but is a result of how you look at the world and at yourself.

'If you look in the mirror and you don't like what you see, don't blame the mirror. If you look at the world and you don't like what you see, don't blame the world'.- Anonymous

Attitude cannot be a mask that you can wear as it goes much deeper than your behaviour in external world. This is what you are at your core and if you are not true to your core it will invariably show. You cannot change your behaviour while your attitude remains the same. Change in your behaviour is simply a change in response to your external environment while a change in attitude is a fundamental shift within you. A change in attitude leads to a change in behaviour but a change in behaviour does not always imply a change in attitude. A change in attitude requires serious and continuous effort towards it over a period of time. It also involves introspection and willingness to make a change for the better. In an interview despite of being at your best behaviour the interviewer can always look through you if your attitude is flawed as behaviour is not a facade that you can put up to hide the real you. Most behavioural valuations have no connection with your behaviour and everything depends wholly on your attitude.

To sum up, attitude is a magnet. If you have a good attitude you will attract good things to yourself while a bad attitude will only lead you to negative experiences. So, try becoming positive and bring more positivity into your life.

❑❑❑

30

Importance of Hobby, Character Building and Motivation in IAS Interview

Hurdles in day-to day life are important to make life interesting, and winning over them makes life meaningful. The profession of civil servant is considered as the most challenging as it is very hectic in nature. They have to take lots of responsibilities at a single time. He/she is bound to face the problem of political interference, corruption, frequent transfers, etc. As it is a 24×7 profession one has to be enthusiastic and stress-free to frame policy as well as to take a decision. One of the best ways to lead a stress-free life is to pursue your hobbies. All hobbies produce psychological benefits. It generates positive feelings and boosts creativity, which enhances the ability to focus and concentrate. It also increases happiness, reduces stress and enhances work performance. Focus generates hormones to retain interest, focus and spark enthusiasm.

Let's make it easier to understand by rewinding your life. During your childhood, you must have got ample of opportunities for pursuing built-in hobbies. Our parents make us for drawing classes, Karate lessons or summer camps. In school, our teacher gives extra credit for those who do extracurricular activities. In college, we cannot think about a life without volunteer activities, arts, and other innovative experiments. When we leave these and start preparing for UPSC exam, we intentionally block the opportunities to pursue hobbies and ultimately it leaves us. But now, the heat waves of the Civil service main exam have come down. The uncertainties regarding how to face interview will be still there under the deepest core of mind. Aspirant should be thorough with his/her DAF. The interview committee members are well experienced in assessing the personality of a candidate. So, the best policy is to remain, to be honest about your bio data. Thoroughly prepare about the hobby you have mentioned in your examination form. Search for popular terms and the basic understanding of that particular hobby, recent happening in that area, etc. Knowledge about current affairs plays a vital role here. One can expect question linked with current affairs. This assesses how dynamic the candidate in his life.

Suppose that if reading is your hobby, then they have the probability to ask – Who is your favourite writer? Which are your favourite novels and why? Do you read a recent novel which might be more popular? What is that book deal with? Even you can expect some technical questions also. For example, if your hobby is photography they may ask you what is the difference between SLR and DSLR is, what is Al Servo? Define Bokeh? What type of photography you do? Are you Paparazzi? Who is Daniel Berehulak? Does a picture destroy or create life? In addition to the direct question, they may ask you, what you would do when you are bored? What will you so during your free time? What will you do when you are alone? These also pose some tricky questions to assess your honesty. Recruiters pose these to check the real character hidden to determine that you would be a good fit for the role personality-wise, as well as by your mains examination marks, skills and knowledge. One should be truthful while answering these questions. It is a great way to impress the panel.

Significance of Hobby

Happiness is in the small pleasures that were feel every day, than in great pieces of good fortune that happen, but seldom, to a man during his lifetime. Youth have a great choice of occupations for their financial happiness but not their mental pleasure. Hobbies pave a way to pursue opportunities. It moulds a man into a living creature.

Hobbies are vital in enriching your viewpoint. Once you start to pursue a new hobby, you open a new chapter in your life. It is a chance to learn new things to enhance your mental efficiency. The more you know, the more you grow. The more you grow you act wisely. Hobbies shift focus from job stress and personal issues. Engaging in enjoyable activities generates self-confidence and motivation, which helps to carry positive performances in aspirant's personal and professional life.

Hobbies belittle the attention from professional stress as well as personal matters. Indulging in entertaining activities kindle self-confidence and keep motivated. The secret of accomplishment is learning how to use pain and pleasure instead of having pain and pleasure use you. If you do that, you're in control of your life. If you don't, life controls you.

There is a big possibility that you will enjoy things as an adult that you have done in past as a kid. Sometimes you might have an awesome coin collection, loved to crawl on a couch with a book and paint crazily. Those are all things you could pick up again as a grownup that would turn out to be great hobby.

One's character proves to be important in choosing hobbies. Some are creative, whereas others desire to be adventurous. Analyse your personality and think about the things you already like and how it can be expanded. Sometimes you may not hit the apt activity for you right out of the gate, but you can have a lot of fun exploring what's out there. Don't be frightened to opt for new things, and soon you will have a hobby that provides you with a lot of fun and an answer to UPSC interview panel.

Do It Daily

A hobby, a day keeps the doldrums away. If you are initiating a new thinking or hobby in your life, it takes time. Post the Civil Service Main examination, you will have ample time in your hands. The best thing is that still you have time and you should start to save the time you spend on social media or watching Television. Carve out a half/an hour daily for exploring your interest and spend it effectively.

'If your actions inspire others to dream more, learn more, do more and become more, you are a leader'.

❑❑❑

31

Why to Become Civil Servants?

The Indian Civil Service (ICS) was constituted after the ratification of the Government of India Act, 1858. The instant need to pass the Act was due to the Indian rebellion of 1857, also known as the Sepoy Mutiny. This new administrative step, in turn, aided in occupying new territories.

Youths, after the India got independent, got attracted by the residual goodwill of ICS, which placed them into the higher echelons of society. The 'social prestige' related with the service became a big attraction and enrolment in the civil service a tour de force.

Primarily, the applicants were drawn from the presidency towns followed with other State capitals. Afterwards, pupils who had education in vernacular medium also joined the service in droves, enriching it, with their comprehensive common sense.

There was an urgent need to stand out in a crowd of 121 crore Indians. Selection into civil service suddenly satisfies this need. To an insecure mind, it offers eternal solace. Shakespeare said that 'Security is mortals' chiefest enemy' and entry into the civil service aids obliterates insecurity.

Jawaharlal Nehru often criticized the ICS for its bent towards British policies. He stated that someone had once said about the ICS, 'with which we are unfortunately still afflicted in this country, as neither Indian, nor civil, nor a service'.

As Prime Minister, he retained the structure and its top people, albeit with a change of title to the 'Indian Administrative Service'.

Does America need a foreign policy for a diplomacy for the 21st century.

Changing Landscape

After introduction of liberalization in India, the All-India Services (AIS) are given the role of a facilitator, and not essentially one of a regulator. This reduced the importance of AIS, and its supremacy in economic decision-making is being encumbered.

In addition, in the next three decades, regional groups by taking over the reins at the State level and the immediacy of the next election drove the agendas of these parties in power.

The AIS officers are made to toe the line of the political bosses. The idea of a 'committed bureaucracy' is being stimulated slightly.

Moreover, the philosophy of society itself is getting transformed. Ill-gotten wealth now imparts instant respectability.

The AIS officials, who always held a ringside opinion of this process of ill-gotten wealth in the Licence-Quota-Permit Raj, initiated working together with political masters. The percentage of officers who are in this collusive collaboration is surging by the day.

The factions in the ruling government favoured civil servants loyal to them. As is seen, from the recent happenings, even 'Lady Officers' have joined the party. It is no more true that women officers are more honest, they have made news for the wrong reasons.

The cardinal ideologies related to civil service, namely, professionalism, anonymity, integrity and neutrality, are slowly diminishing.

The principles with which the AIS unites itself are self-acquired, the links were missing at the entry, the links are slowly forged and the chains formed. The process seemed to be full of compromises, both intellectual and fiscal.

Civil servants joining politics is a loathsome spectacle. One even became a Chief Minister. This development severally compromises neutrality during their tenure in service. Usually, civil servants were sent as Governors, post-retirement. Now even for this honour, civil servants are helping politicians unabashedly. Most of the evils perpetuated by 'to-retire' civil servants are their craving for post-retirement sinecures.

As said by Ronald Reagan: 'politics is supposed to be the second oldest profession; I have come to realize that it bears a very close resemblance to the first'. Possibly, had he operated with the AIS closely, he would have extended the comparison with civil servants also.

Vinod Mehta, in his book The Lucknow Boy, praises E.A.S. Sarma, who confronted the PMO to uphold steadfastly what, he assumed, was in the larger interest of the country.

In recent times, in Andhra Pradesh, some officials who weathered the onslaught of a former CM are breathing easy, and their descendants who obeyed the 'diktats' of the former CM are facing the CBI probe.

Noam Chomsky, in his book Deterring Democracy, expected that the unholy businessman-politician link will harm democracy. No party is wholesome, now, without the media. The politician-business-media house link, with the tentacles in the bureaucratic network, is a heady mix. Now, well heeled, highly-networked women in the media coalesced into business groups and when caught, vociferously pleaded an 'error of judgment' and escaped. Where does this leave the civil services — in the fox holes?

Judicial activism is one more dimension that has gained popularity over the years. Now, a few high-profile cases against the AIS get so much adverse publicity that it becomes a feed forward mechanism for the judiciary to engage in more activism.

Ralph Waldo Emerson said 'the only person you are destined to become is the person you decide to be'. The future of civil services is directly dependent on the principles followed by present civil servants.. Unless we faithfully return to the old edicts of professionalism, anonymity, integrity and neutrality, the evanescent goodwill will be a dream.

Silent hard work is of utmost importance in recent times. One should leave the system unheard, unsung and unwept and while in the system one should be free, fair and frank.

It is apt to recall the most famous 'Pogo' quotation at this moment: 'we have met the enemy and he is us'. The civil servants we wish 'to be or not to be' are within us. ❑❑❑

32

Most Significant Guidelines to Prepare for Civil Services Examination

1. ***Knowing the commission:*** Every candidate should have sufficient and apt knowledge about the organizations and subsets of IAS and all India services. IAS, IPS and IFS (Indian Forest Service) compose All India Service, whereas the subsets of CSE include elite services such as IRS (revenue service), IFS (foreign service), IIS (information service), etc.

   To clear these exams is not an easy challenge. One has to bring several changes while preparing for the popular exam.

   Speaking about selecting civil servants, IGP Robin Hibu, IPS batch 1993, said, 'First should be compulsory rigorous aptitude test by impartial team. Secondly, a specialized services with all holistic regular training with robust accountability and delegation of power on young civil servants'.

2. ***Clear conscience:*** Before initiating a preparation for civil services, one should have a proper idea on why he/she wanted to be a civil servant.

   'Let the top brains of our youth do critical analysis before plunging into this much so call hallowed civil services. In today's liberalized India, we need more entrepreneurs, NRI, technocrats. The best should not be groomed to be Babus alone'. —IGP Robin Hibu, IPS 1993.

3. ***Organized preparation:*** Before facing the exam, aspirants need to have a deep understanding of the basics of several subjects and discipline of studies. Ranging from the elementary quantitative ability to the core of governance, from climatology to oceanography, from agriculture to economy, from science to modern technology, every successful candidate must have attained the basic knowledge and forged with perseverance, patience, rationality, integrity and leadership quality.

To acquire sufficient knowledge, it is suggested that one should break the subject topic-wise and prepare according to one's convenience.

4. ***Think like a policy maker:*** The secret behind the success in civil services is not only concentrating on books alone, but also improving logical reasoning and rationality. Otherwise no amount of knowledge and guidance can earn you the confidence to face the great trial.

   For instance, the question in 2016 prelims GS paper-1 regarding the Atal Pension Yojana, a scheme for the unorganized sector, is a best example of how grasping the notion alone could supplement the slightest knowledge one has already acquired. Each person is a portion of the governance and the questions on governance and economy are directly or indirectly related. To best understand the idea of CSE, you must think like the policy maker, the street vendor, the analyst, the observer and the beneficiary.

5. ***Time management:*** Managing your time will provide to be a most important aspect for attaining success. To master time management, regular practice and mock tests are advised by the experienced people.

❑❑❑

33

Five Good Reasons to Opt for Civil Services as a Career

1. ***Respect:*** Civil service is regarded as one of the most respected job options since the inception of governance. Rome, in a pre-empire period, was a republic with a history of long democratic rule.
2. ***Decent pay and stipends:*** Civil servants enjoy a handsome salary and various allowances from the government.
3. ***All India service:*** One can fulfil his/her desire to serve the country after being selected as IAS.
4. ***An agent of change:*** Being deputed as district magistrate, district collector or district commissioner, one is vested with the responsibilities to initiate changes and educate the masses by providing the best need services and measures for the masses.
5. ***Insightfulness:*** What freedom is more glorious than the freedom from ignorance?

'It's an opportunity in the true sense to directly serve the people, only if you are truly motivated to serve the people. However, I would advice, don't join only for sake of prestige, money or comfort. In spite of having all limitations, aspirants can make a difference. Having said that personally, I feel, there should be complete overhaul of our steel frame of civil services. I wish to see my country as possessing robust and specialized civil services in key sectors'.

–IGP Robin Hibu, IPS 1993.

Part of a Civil Servant in Governance

According to Max Weber, bureaucracy is an art of administration and dominance over governance through knowledge. Similarly, the responsibility of a civil servant is to elevate the society, spread awareness, battle with corruption, uphold social and cultural harmony, eliminate superstitious beliefs, support social and economic equality, augment the education system and act as the direct representative of the government.

An IAS officer has immense scope to serve the society in so many ways. There is no index to measure how much the administrators can help the masses.

❑❑❑

34

Best Mindset While Preparing for Civil Services Interview

If you desire to become a doctor, you should imagine being in the shoes of one. To some extent, it assists in understanding the hurdles and the pluses. Likewise, you can attempt to visualize yourself as a Civil Servant even while preparing for the exams, as that can (to some extent) help you raise the bar from time to time.

Avoid the Extremes: 'All politicians are corrupt. All judges are lazy and slow. All policemen are brutal. All teachers are idiots. All businessmen are profit-hungry'. If you have thoughts like this, your preparations for IAS are on a wrong way. This is so because India has had exceptions to the above in all fields. It's only that you haven't read enough to discover those names. Think extreme → Write extreme → Look like an extremist → Fail for sure.

Accept the Truth: Our personal thoughts can, sometimes, override our decision in many subjects. For instance, most Indians think Pakistanis are bad people, and there is no hope for Indo-Pak relations. But look back, and you'll discover that our stock is the same. We all descended from the Indus Valley civilization originally. So if they are bad, we are perhaps bad too. A better statement could be – 'Pakistan is a horrible State, though most Pakistanis must be good people, as people are, everywhere'. This is a positive way of looking at a rather despondent situation!

Take a Moment to Think: The capability and longing of young Indians to answer a question even before it is fully asked is fabulous. And that's where they frequently fumble. Do not hurry that much. Go a bit slow. Let the question be completed. Take a deep breath. Let a few seconds pass by. Then come up with your answer. You'll be astonished by the beauty and well-formed nature of your own answers, rather than the hurried mish-mash you'd have otherwise expressed. This will save you during interviews, and will surely help you produce better answers in the Mains.

Reduce your Ego: The duty of a civil servant is to serve the people and the government, not to question it.

Make Virtue and Wealth: Do not get slowed down by the above point. It does not mean that you are permitted to exercise your originality. In reality, quite the contrary! If you show a lot of positive enthusiasm and creativity, while keeping your tongue under a strong leash, then the political bosses or your bureaucracy seniors will consider you as a 'person of solutions'. Your guidance and ideas will be sought every time they need to think laterally. A good example is Mr. Amitabh Kant, the brain behind the Make in India programme of Mr. Modi.

Live like a Senior Civil Servant: Get up early. Get ready quickly. Start your work soon. Work hard attentively whole day. Take a small lunch break. Don't take a fag at work. Don't gossip. Read a lot. Clear today's work today. Get ready for tomorrow. Seek others' help if needed. Smile. Solve. Seek.

❑❑❑

35

Decoding Interview

An interview is a process of two-way communication between two or more people where the interviewer interrogates the interviewee to elicit facts or statements. Interviews are a basic part of journalism and media reporting, but are also used in many other circumstances, including qualitative research. In journalism, interviews are one of the most important methods used to gather information, and present views to readers, listeners or viewers.

Interview as a Method for Judging Character

The qualitative research interview intends to define the connotations of central themes in the life world of the subjects. The main theme in interviewing is to recognize the meaning of what the interviewees say. To make it more understandable, see Jaber F. Gubrium and James A. Holstein's (2002) 'Handbook of Interview Research'. For a deconstruction of subjectivity in the interview, see James A. Holstein and Jaber F. Gubrium (1995) 'The Active Interview'. Interviewing, when measured as a method for conducting qualitative research, is a procedure used to realize the experiences of others. Interviewing is different from other approaches of data gathering in that it is often more exploratory in nature, and permits for more flexibility. Interviewing stems from the desire to know more about the people around us and to better understand how the people around us view the world we live in: 'At the heart of interviewing research is an interest in other individuals' stories because they are of worth'. Therefore, interviewing is most impactful when the aim of said research is to gain insight into the 'subjective understanding' of those around us. By asking members 'why', we are in a position to not only observe their behaviour but to subsequently recognize the meaning that underlies that behaviour, and to have this meaning explained to us in the participant's own words It is a much debated topic in fields that study households whether interviews should be conducted individually or collectively (e.g. as couple interviews).

Features of Qualitative Research Interviews

- Interviews are done by the interviewer on the basis of what the interviewee reveals.
- Interviews are more personal in nature than questionnaires.
- In the personal interview, the interviewer deals openly with the interviewee.
- In contrast to mail surveys, the interviewer has the chance to investigate or ask follow-up questions.
- Interviews are generally easier for the interviewee, especially if what is sought are opinions and/or impressions.
- Interviews are time consuming and they are resource intensive.
- The interviewer is considered a part of the measurement instrument and interviewer has to be well trained in how to respond to any contingency.
- Interview offers a chance of face-to-face communication between two persons; hence, it reduces conflicts.

Technique

When opting for interview as a procedure to conduct qualitative research, it is vital to be tactful and sensitive in your approach. Interviewer and researcher, Irving Seidman, devotes an entire chapter of his book, Interviewing as Qualitative Research, to the import of proper interviewing technique and interviewer etiquette. Some of the essentials of his skill are summarized below:

- ***Listening:*** As per Seidman, this is the most important quality required in interviewing. Moreover, interviewers must be ready to listen on three different levels: they must listen to what the participant is actually saying, they must listen to the 'inner voice' or subtext of what the participant is communicating, and they must also listen to the process and flow of the interview so as to remain aware of how tired or bored the participant is as well as logistics such as how much time has already passed and how many questions still remain. The listening skills required in an interview require more focus and attention to detail than what is typical in normal conversation. Thus, it is often supportive for interviewers to take notes while the participant answers the.

- ***Ask questions (to follow up and to clarify):*** Although an interviewer usually enters each interview with a prearranged, standardized set of questions, it is vital that they also put up follow-up questions throughout the process. Such questions might inspire a participant to elaborate upon something poignant that they've shared and are important in acquiring a more comprehensive understanding of the subject matter. Besides, it is important that an interviewer ask clarifying questions when they are confused. If the narrative, details, or chronology of a participant's responses become unclear, it is often suitable for the interviewer to enquire them about these aspects of their story so as to keep their transcriptions accurate.
- ***Be respectful of limits:*** Seidman describes this technique as 'Explore, don't probe'. It is important that while the participants are being interviewed, they should be motivated to explore their experiences in a manner that is sensitive and respectful. They should not be 'probed' in such a way that makes them feel uncomfortable or like a specimen in lab. If too much time is spent dwelling on minute details or if too many follow-up questions are asked, it is possible that the participant will become defensive or unwilling to share. Therefore, it is the interviewer's goal to maintain a balance between ambiguity and specificity in their question asking.
- ***Avoid leading questions:*** Leading questions refer to queries which suggest or imply an answer. Although they are frequently asked innocently, they run the risk of altering the validity of the responses obtained as they discourage interviewees from using their own language to describe their sentiments. Thus it is preferable that interviewers ask open-ended questions instead. For instance, instead of asking 'Did the experience

make you feel sad?' – which seems to be a leading question – it would be better to ask 'How did the experience make you feel?' – as this asks for no expectation.

- ***Don't intrude:*** Interviewee should be at ease respected during the interview. Thus, interviewers should avoid interrupting participants whenever possible. While participants may digress in their responses and while the interviewer may lose interest in what they are saying at one point or another, it is important that they be thoughtful in their attempts to keep the participant on track and to return to the subject matter in question.
- ***Make the participant feel comfortable:*** Interviewing creates an environment where a participant is quizzed to reveal personal or emotional information in the presence of a complete stranger. Thus, many interviewers find it helpful to ask the participant to address them as if they were 'someone else', such as a close friend or family member. This is often an impactful process for tuning into the aforementioned 'inner voice' of the participant and breaking down the more presentational barriers of the guarded 'outer voice' which frequently prevails.

Strengths and Weaknesses

Although there are many methods of interviewing, qualitative interviewing is no doubt a winner in all aspects. Possibly the greatest benefit of qualitative interviewing is the depth of detail from the interviewee. Interviewing participants can paint a picture of what happened in a specific event, tell us their perspective of such event, as well as give other social cues. Social cues, such as voice, intonation, body language etc. of the interviewee can give the interviewer a lot of extra information that can be added to the verbal answer of the interviewee on a question. The extent of description, whether it be verbal or nonverbal, can reveal an otherwise hidden interrelatedness between emotions, people and objects unlike many quantitative methods of research. Besides, qualitative interviewing has an exclusive advantage in its specific form. Researchers can modify the queries they ask to the participant to get rich, full stories and the information they need for their project. They can make it clear to the respondent when they need more examples or explanations. Not only can researchers also learn about specific events, they can also gain insight into people's interior experiences, specifically how people perceive and how they interpreted their perceptions. How events had an effect on their thoughts and feelings. In this, researchers can comprehend the process of an event instead of what just happened and how they reacted to it. Another benefit of qualitative interviewing is what it can provide the readers of academic journals and papers. Research can write a clearer report to their readers, giving them a 'fuller understanding of the experiences of our respondents and a greater chance to identify with the respondent, if only briefly'.

It can also be said that qualitative interviewing is not a perfect method for all types of research. It does have its drawbacks also. First, there can be problems with the preparation of the interview. Not only is recruiting people for interviews hard, due to the typically personal nature of the interview, planning where to meet them and when can be difficult. Participants can cancel or change the meeting place at the last minute. During the actual interview, a possible weakness is missing some information. This can arise from the immense multitasking that the interviewer must do. Not only do they have to make the respondent feel very comfortable, they have to keep as much eye contact as possible, write down as much as they can, and think of follow up questions. Post interview, the procedure of coding starts and along comes its own set of disadvantages. First, coding can be extremely time consuming. This process usually needs multiple people, which can also become expensive. Second, the nature of qualitative research itself doesn't lend itself very well to quantitative analysis. Some investigators report more missing data in interview research than survey research; therefore, it can be difficult to compare populations.

How it feels to be a Participant in Qualitative Research Interviews

In contrast to something like a written survey, interviews provides a considerably higher degree of familiarity, with participants often conveying personal details to their interviewers in a real-time, face-to-face setting. As such, this technique can evoke an array of significant feelings and experiences within those being interviewed. On the positive side, interviewing can offer participants with an outlet to express themselves. Since the goal of interviewers is to learn, not to treat or counsel, they do not offer participants any advice, but nonetheless, telling an attentive listener about concerns and cares can be pleasing. As qualitative researcher Robert S. Weiss states, 'To talk to someone who listens, and listens closely, can be valuable, because one's own experience, through the process of being voiced and shared, is validated'.

Such validation, however, can have a disadvantage if an interviewee feels discouraged upon end of the interview relationship, for, unlike with figures like therapists or counsellors, interviewers do not take a measure of ongoing responsibility for the participant, and their association is for short term. To minimize the potential for this disappointment, researchers should tell participants how many interviews they will be conducting in advance, and also provide them with some type of closure, such as a research summary or a copy of the project publication. On the negative side, the multiple-question-based interviews can make participants feel uncomfortable and encroached upon if an interviewer goes on territory that they feel is too personal or private. To avoid crossing this line, researchers should try to differentiate between public information and private information, and only delve deeper into private information after attempting to gauge a participant's comfort level in discussing it.

Additionally, the comparatively friendly nature of interviews can make interviewees feel vulnerable to harm or exploitation. This can be especially true for circumstances in which a superior interviews a subordinate, like when teacher interviewers his or her student. In these circumstances, participants may be fearful of providing a 'wrong answer', or saying something that could potentially get them into trouble and reflect on them negatively. However, all interview relations, not just clearly superior-subordinate ones, are determined by some degree of inequality, as interviewers and participants want and receive different things from the technique. Thus, researchers should always be concerned with the potential for participant feelings of vulnerability, especially in situations where personal information is revealed. To tackle such feelings of vulnerability and inequity and to make participants feel at ease, researchers should make them aware about the study, such as who is running it and what potential risks it might entail, and also with information about their rights, such as the right to review interview materials and withdraw from the process at any time. It is especially important that researchers always emphasize the voluntary nature of participating in a study so that the participants remain aware of their agency. These above-mentioned power dynamics prevailing in interviews can also have definite effects on different social groups depending on the racial background, gender, age and class. Race, for instance, can create issues in an interview setting if participants of a marginalized racial background are quizzed by white researchers, in which case the reality of historical and societal prejudices can create a sense of scepticism and distrust. Gender dynamics can similarly affect feelings, with men sometimes acting overbearingly when interviewing women and acting dismissively when being interviewed by women, and same-gendered pairs being vulnerable to false assumptions of commonality or a sense of implicit competition. In case of class, interviewees of supposed lower status exhibit, in some cases, either excessive scepticism or excessive submissiveness, and in terms of age, children and seniors may demonstrate fears of being patronized.

To eradicate these social group-related pessimist feelings, interviewers should remain delicate towards possible sources of such tensions, and act accordingly by underlining good manners, respect and a genuine interest in the participant, all of which can help bridge social barriers.

In the end, another facet of interviews that can impact how an interviewee feels is how the interviewer states his or her own feelings, for researchers can project their moods and emotions onto those they are interviewing. For example, if an interviewer feels noticeably uncomfortable, the participant may start to share this discomfort, and if an interviewer exhibits anger, he or she is in danger of passing it on to the participant. So, researchers should try to be calm, polite and interested at all times.

Psychosocial and Psychoanalytic Methods to Interviewing

Hollway and Jefferson constituted a procedure of researching motivated by psychoanalysis where the participant's defence mechanisms were considered. They framed the 'Free Association Narrative Interview' which, somewhat analogous to free association in clinical psychoanalysis, is categorized as unstructured dialogue, and considering that the relations of the participants, sometimes seemingly irrelevant, may in fact link to the research question. This process has been used in relation research interviews on the topic of migration.

❑❑❑

36

Understanding the Types of Interviews

Informal, Conversational Interview

This includes questions that are not predetermined questions so as to remain as open and adaptable as possible to the interviewee's nature and priorities; while interviewing, the interviewer 'goes with the flow'.

General Interview Guide Approach

This type of interview is focused to guarantee that the same general areas of information are collected from each interviewee; this offers more focus than the conversational approach, but still permits a degree of freedom and adaptability in extracting the information from the interviewee.

Standardized, Open-ended Interview

This type of interview includes same open-ended questions for all interviewees; this method facilitates faster interviews that can be more easily analysed and compared.

Closed, Fixed-response Interview

In this type of interview, all interviewees are posed with the same questions and asked to select answers from among the same set of alternatives. This method is useful for those not practiced in interviewing.

Interviewer's Judgements

As per Hackman and Oldman, several aspects can form an interviewer's judgement about a job applicant. However, these aspects can be minimized by training interviews to recognize them. Some examples are given as under:

Prior Information

Interviewers generally attain some prior information about job aspirants, such as recruiter evaluations, application blanks, online screening results or the merits of psychological tests. This can help the interviewer to form a favourable or unfavourable attitude towards applicants before meeting them.

The Contrast Effect

How the interviewers assess a specific applicant may depend on their standards of comparison, that is, the features of the applicants they interviewed previously.

Interviewers' Prejudices

This can happen when the interviewers' conclusion is their personal likes and dislikes. These may include but are not limited to racial and ethnic background, applicants who show certain potentials or traits and refuse to consider their abilities or characteristics.

Employment-Related Interviews

- Exit interview
- Informational interview
- Job interview
    - Case interview
    - Programming interview
- Microsoft interview
- Telephone interview

Other Types of Interviews

- Cognitive interview
- Computer-assisted personal vs. telephone interviewing
- Investigative interview

- Ladder interview
- Mall-intercept personal interview
- Mock Interview
- Multiple mini interview
- Online interview
- Parent-teacher interview
- Psychiatric interview
- Reference interview, between a librarian and a library user
- Repertory grid interview
- Structured, semi-structured, and unstructured interview
- Structured Clinical Interview for DSM-IV

Different Phases of Interview Investigation

- Thermalizing, the why and what of the investigation
- Designing, plan the design of the study
- Interviewing, conduct the interview based on a guide
- Transcribing, prepare the interview material for analysis
- Analysing, decide on the purpose, the topic, the nature and methods of analysis that are appropriate
- Verifying, ascertain the validity of the interview findings
- Reporting, reveal findings of the study based on academic criteria.

❑❑❑

37

Significance of Mock Interview

A mock interview refers to imitation of an interview used for the purpose of trainings. The interview makes an attempt to resemble a real interview as closely as possible, and provides experience for the candidate. The mock interview helps the job applicant learn what is expected in a job interview, and improves the applicant's self-presentation. Mock interviews are often videotaped, and the candidate is shown the tape after the session, along with feedback from the interviewer. The mock interview coach will provide constructive feedback on all aspects of the interview process. Mock interviews are most common for job interviews, but may also be used to train people to handle journalists. The mock interview coach will try to make the interview as realistic as possible. Many of the questions asked are interview questions from actual employers. The mock interview and critique will last approximately one hour. The mock interview takes about 20 minutes, then the job seeker and coach watch the interview and discuss the job seeker's performance. The mock interview coach's level of direct experience in the industry or field of interest for the job seeker can make the mock interview more or less effective. This is the case because mock interview coaches can best help job seekers when they have insights into what hiring managers are looking for and can gauge how well job seekers are answering the questions. While there are many career coaches who provide a full suite of services to help job seekers figure out their career path, niche websites exist that focus on helping job seekers with their interviewing skills. Examples of these sites include Prept and Evisors. The mock interview focuses on self-knowledge, past experiences, knowledge of the industry the applicant wishes to enter, and how well the applicant can convey that information. The job seeker gains the most experience from the mock interview if it is treated as an actual interview. The mock interview is a safe place to practice interview skills and gain feedback. It is also an area to gain the confidence and experience of giving an actual employment interview. This is also conducted in companies with a purpose to address clients with confidence and learn those things which are needed for the meeting.

□□□

38

Significance of Interview

Nonverbal communication comprises of two-thirds of all communication. Nonverbal communication can depict a message both verbally and with the right body signals. Body signals comprise of physical features, conscious and unconscious gestures and signals, and the mediation of personal space. The wrong message can be framed if the body language conveyed does not show any similarity with a verbal message. Nonverbal communication strengthens a first impression in common situations like attracting a partner or in a business interview: impressions are on average formed within the first four seconds of contact. First encounters or interactions with another person strongly affect a person's perception. When the other person or group is absorbing the message, they concentrate on the whole environment around them, meaning the other person makes use of all five senses in the interaction: 83% sight, 11% hearing, 3% smell, 2% touch along with 1% taste.

Initial Impression

It takes merely one-tenth of a second for someone to evaluate and make the first impression. The first impression is a deep-rooted non-verbal communicator. The way a person portrays themselves on the first encounter is non-verbal statement to the observer. 'First impressions are lasting impressions'. There can be positive and negative impressions. Positive impressions can be made through the way you present yourself. Presentation can include clothing, piercings, tattoos, and other visible attributes. Negative impressions can also be based on presentation and also on personal prejudice. However, first impressions, sometimes, can be misleading, can on many occasions be an accurate depiction of others.

Posture

There are several different types of body positioning to show certain postures, including slouching, towering, legs spread, jaw thrust, shoulders forward and arm crossing. The posture or bodily stance shown by individuals communicates a variety of messages whether good or bad. Posture can be made use of to ascertain a participant's degree of attention or involvement, the difference in status between communicators, and the level of fondness a person has for the other communicator, depending on body 'openness'. Studies finding the effect of posture on interpersonal relationships show that mirror-image congruent postures, where one person's left side is parallel to the other person's right side, leads to favourable perception of communicators and positive speech; a person who shows a forward lean or reduces a backward lean also signifies positive sentiment while communicating.

Posture can be situation-relative, that is, people will bring changes in their posture based on the situation they are in.

Clothing

Clothing is one of the most common forms of non-verbal communication. The study of clothing and other objects as a means of non-verbal communication is known as artifactics or objectics. The types of clothing that an individual wears conveys nonverbal cues about his or her personality, background and financial status, and how others will respond to them. An individual's clothing style can demonstrate their culture, mood, level of confidence, interests, age, authority, values/beliefs, and their sexual identity. For example, Jewish men may wear yamakas to outwardly communicate their religious belief. Similarly, clothing can communicate what nationality a person or group is, for example, in traditional festivities Scottish men often wear kilts to specify their culture. Aside from communicating a person's beliefs and nationality, clothing can be used as a nonverbal cue to attract others. Men and women may shower themselves with accessories and high-end fashion in order to attract partners they are interested in. In this case, clothing is used as a form of self-expression in which people can flaunt their power, wealth, sex appeal, or creativity. A study of the clothing worn by women attending discothèques, carried out in Vienna, Austria, showed that in certain groups of women (particularly women who were without their partners), motivation for sex and levels of sexual hormones were correlated with aspects of their clothing, particularly the amount of skin displayed and the presence of sheer clothing.

Gestures

Gestures can usually be made with help of hands, arms or body, and these also include the movements of the head, face and eyes, for example winking, nodding or rolling one's eyes. Although the study of gesture is still in its infancy, some broad categories of gestures have been identified by researchers. The most familiar are the so-called emblems or quotable gestures. These are conventional, culture-specific gestures that can be used as replacement for words, such as the hand wave used in western cultures for 'hello' and 'goodbye'. A single emblematic gesture can have a very different significance in different cultural contexts, ranging from complimentary to highly offensive. For a list of emblematic gestures, see List of gestures. There are a few universal gestures such as the shoulder shrug.

Gestures can also be classified as either speech independent or speech related. Speech-independent gestures depend on culturally accepted interpretation and have a direct verbal translation. A wave or a peace sign are examples of speech-independent gestures. Speech-related gestures are used in parallel with verbal speech; this form of nonverbal communication is used to emphasize the message that is being communicated. Speech-related gestures are intended to provide supplemental information to a verbal message such as pointing to an object of discussion. Facial expressions, more than anything, serve as a practical means of communication. With all the various muscles that precisely control mouth, lips, eyes, nose, forehead, and jaw, human faces are estimated to be capable of more than ten thousand different expressions. This versatility makes non-verbals of the face extremely efficient and honest, unless deliberately manipulated. Besides, many of these emotions, including happiness, sadness, anger, fear, surprise, disgust, shame, anguish and interest are universally identified. Displays of emotions can generally be categorized into two groups: negative and positive. Negative emotions usually manifest as increased tension in various muscle groups: tightening of jaw muscles, furrowing of forehead, squinting eyes, or lip occlusion (when the lips seemingly disappear). In contrast, positive emotions are revealed by the loosening of the furrowed lines on the forehead, relaxation of the muscles around the mouth, and widening of the eye area. When individuals are truly relaxed and at ease, the head will also tilt to the side, exposing our most vulnerable area, the neck. This is a high-comfort display, usually seen during courtship, which is almost impossible to mimic when tense or suspicious.

Gestures can be categorized into three groups:

- ***Adapters:*** Some hand movements are not considered to be gestures. They consist of manipulations either of the person or some object (e.g. clothing, pencils, and eyeglasses) – the kinds of scratching, fidgeting, rubbing, tapping, and touching that people often do with their hands. Such behaviours are referred to as adapters. They may not be perceived as meaningfully related to the speech in which they accompany, but may serve as the basis for dispositional inferences of the speaker's emotion (nervous, uncomfortable, and bored).
- ***Gestures through symbols:*** Other hand movements are perceived as gestures. They are movements with specific, conventionalized meanings called symbolic gestures. Familiar symbolic gestures include the 'raised fist', 'bye-bye', and 'thumbs up'. In contrast to adapters, symbolic gestures are used intentionally and serve a clear communicative function. Every culture has their own set of gestures, some of which are unique only to a specific culture. Very similar gestures can have very different meanings across cultures. Gestures through symbols are generally used in the absence of speech, but can also accompany speech.
- ***Gestures through conversation:*** Conversational gestures occupy the middle ground between adapters and symbolic

gestures. These gestures do not refer to actions or words, but do accompany speech. Conversational gestures are hand movements that accompany speech, and are related to the speech they accompany. Though they do accompany speech, conversational gestures are not observed in the absence of speech and are only made by an individual who is speaking.

Eye Contact

Eye contact is the instance when two people pass a glance at each other's eyes simultaneously; it is the main nonverbal way of indicating engagement, interest, attention and involvement. Studies have found that people use their eyes to indicate interest. This includes frequently recognized actions of winking and movements of the eyebrows. Disinterest is highly noticeable when little or no eye contact is made a social setting. When an individual is interested however, the pupils will dilate. According to Eckman, 'Eye contact (also called mutual gaze) is another major channel of nonverbal communication. The duration of eye contact is its most meaningful aspect'. Generally speaking, the longer there is established eye contact between two people, the greater the intimacy levels. Gaze includes the actions of looking while talking and listening. The length of a gaze, the frequency of glances, patterns of fixation, pupil dilation, and blink rate are all vital cues in nonverbal communication. 'Liking generally increases as mutual gazing increases'.

Apart from the detection of disinterest, deceit can also be seen in a person. Hogan states 'when someone is being deceptive their eyes tend to blink a lot more. Eyes act as leading indicator of truth or deception', Both nonverbal and verbal cues are beneficial while detecting deception. It is typical for people who are detecting lies to rely consistently on verbal cues but this can hinder how well they detect deception. Those who are lying and those who are telling the truth possess different forms of nonverbal and verbal cues and this is important to keep in mind. In addition, it is important to note that understanding the cultural background of a person will influence how easily deception is detectable because nonverbal cues may differ depending on the culture. In addition to eye contact these nonverbal cues can consist of physiological aspects including pulse rate as well as levels of perspiration. Besides, eye aversion can be predictive of deception. Eye aversion is the avoidance of eye contact. Eye contact and facial expressions offer important social and emotional information. On a whole, as Pease states, 'Give the amount of eye contact that makes everyone feel comfortable. Unless looking at others is a cultural no-no, lookers gain more credibility than non-lookers'.

In case of concealing deception, nonverbal communication makes it easier to lie without getting revealed. This is the conclusion of a study where people watched made-up interviews of persons accused of having stolen a wallet. The interviewees lied in about 50% of the cases. People had access to either written transcript of the interviews, or audio tape recordings, or video recordings. The more clues that were available to those watching, the larger was the trend that interviewees who actually lied were judged to be truthful. That is, people that are clever at lying can use voice tone and face expression to give the impression that they are truthful. Contrary to popular belief, a liar does not always avoid eye contact. In an attempt to be more convincing, liars deliberately made more eye contact with interviewers than those that were telling the truth. However, there are many cited examples of cues to deceit, delivered via nonverbal (Para verbal and visual) communication channels, through which deceivers supposedly unwittingly provide clues to their concealed knowledge or actual opinions. Many studies investigating the nonverbal cues to deceit rely upon human coding of video footage, although a latest study also showed bodily movement differences between truth-tellers and liars with the use of an automated body motion capture system.

□□□

39

Significance of Bio-Data or Curriculum Vitae

A curriculum vitae (CV) gives a sketch of work experience and other qualifications of a person. In a few countries, a CV is typically the first item that a potential employer encounters regarding the job seeker and is typically used to screen applicants, often followed by an interview, when looking for employment.

Applications

In the United Kingdom, many Commonwealth countries and Ireland, a CV is short (usually a maximum of two sides of A4 paper), and therefore contains only a summary of the job seeker's employment history, qualifications and some personal information. It is usually updated to alter the emphasis of the information as per the specific position for which the job seeker is applying. Many CVs contain keywords that potential employers might pick up on and display the content in the most flattering manner, brushing over information like poor grades. A CV can also be extended to include an extra page for the job-seeker's publications if these are important for the job. In the United States, a CV is used in academic circles and medical careers as a 'replacement' for a résumé and is far more comprehensive; the term résumé is used for most recruitment campaigns. A CV discusses about education, publications and other achievements to a greater extent than a résumé, but it is often expected that professionals use a short CV that focuses their current academic lives and not compulsorily their full history.

Etymology and Spellings

Curriculum vitae is a Latin expression which may be loosely defined as [the] course of [my] life. In today's usage, curriculum is less marked as a foreign loanword. Traditionally the word vitae is rendered in English using the ligature æ, hence vitæ, although this convention is less common in contemporary practice. The plural of curriculum vitae, in Latin, is formed following Latin rules of grammar as curricula vitae (meaning 'courses of life')—not curriculum vita (which is grammatically incorrect) and not curricula vitarum. The form vitae is the singular genitive of vita and is translated as 'of life'. In English, the plural of the full expression curriculum vitae is seldom used; the plural of curriculum on its own is often written as 'curricula' instead of the traditional curriculums.

Significance of Résumé

A résumé refers to a document used by individuals to present their backgrounds and skills. Résumés can be used for a variety of purposes, but usually they are used to secure new employment. A typical résumé comprises of a summary of relevant job experience and education. The résumé is usually one of the first items, along with a cover letter and sometimes an application for employment, which a potential employer sees regarding the job seeker and is typically used to screen applicants, often followed by an interview. The résumé is comparable to a curriculum vitae (CV) in many countries. However, it is substantially shorter as compared to a CV in English Canada, the U.S. and Australia. In French, résumé refers to summary or synopsis.

❖ Description

In multiple contexts, a résumé is short (often one to three pages), and directs a reader's attention to those aspects of a person's background that are directly relevant to a particular position. Many résumés consist of keywords that potential employers are looking for, make heavy use of active verbs and present content in a flattering manner. A résumé refers to a marketing tool in which the content should be adapted to suit each individual job application and/or applications aimed at a specific industry. The transmission of résumés directly to employers became increasingly popular as late as 2002. Job seekers were able to circumvent the job application process and reach employers through direct email contact and résumé blasting, a term meaning the mass distribution of résumés to increase personal visibility within the job market. However the mass distribution of résumés to employers can often have a negative effect on the applicant's chances of securing employment as the résumés tend not to be tailored for the specific positions the applicant is applying for. It is usually therefore more sensible to adjust the résumé for each position applied for. The complexity or simplicity of various résumé formats tends to produce results varying from person to person, for the occupation, and to the industry. It is important to note that résumés or CVs used by medical professionals, professors, artists and people in other specialized fields may be comparatively longer. For example, an artist's résumé, typically excluding any non-art-related employment, may include extensive lists of solo and group exhibitions. Interestingly, when employers go through a résumé, they typically only spend ten to fifteen seconds, thus the top half of a résumé is the prime real estate for significant information.

❖ Styles

A simple résumé is a synopsis typically limited to one or two pages of size A4 or Letter-size, focusing only those experiences and qualifications that the author considers most relevant to the desired position. Academic CVs in the US are typically longer. Résumés may be organized in different ways. Some of the more common formats are as follows:

Reverse Chronological Résumé

A reverse chronological résumé comprises of job experiences a candidate in reverse chronological order, generally covering the previous 10 to 15 years. Positions are listed with starting and ending dates. Current positions on a résumé typically list the starting date to the present or to the current year. Both are considered acceptable. The reverse chronological résumé format is most commonly used by those who are not professional résumé writers. In using this format, the main body of the document becomes the Professional

Experience section, starting from the most recent experience and moving chronologically backwards through a succession of previous experience. The reverse chronological résumé works to build credibility through experience gained, while illustrating career growth over time and filling all gaps in a career trajectory. A chronological résumé is not suggested to job seekers with gaps in their career summaries. In the United Kingdom, the chronological résumé is likely to extend only as far back as the applicant's GCSE/Standard Grade qualifications.

Functional Résumé

A functional résumé comprises of work experience and skills sorted by skill or job functional area.

The functional résumé mainly focuses on skills that are specific to the type of position being sought. This format directly emphasizes specific professional capabilities and utilizes experience summaries as its primary means of communicating professional competency. In contrast, the chronological résumé format will briefly highlight these competencies prior to presenting a comprehensive timeline of career growth through reverse chronological listings, with the most recent experience listed first. The functional résumé works well for those making a career change, having a varied work history or with little work experience. A functional résumé is also preferred for applications to jobs that require very specific skills or clearly defined personality traits. A functional résumé is a good method for highlighting particular skills or experiences, especially when those particular skills or experiences may have derived from a role which was held some time ago. Rather than concentrating on the length of time that has passed, the functional résumé helps the reader to recognize those skills quickly.

Hybrid Résumé

The hybrid résumé makes a balance between the functional and chronological approaches. A résumé organized this way typically leads with a functional list of job skills, followed by a chronological list of employers. The hybrid résumé has a tendency to repeat itself and is, therefore, less widely used than the other two.

Online Résumés

Due to the advent of Internet, it has brought about a new era for the résumé. As the search for employment has become more electronic, résumés have followed suit. It is common for employers only to accept résumés electronically, either out of practicality or preference. This electronic boom has changed much about the way résumés are written, read, and processed. Many employers, and recruitment agencies working on their behalf, insist on receiving résumés in a particular file format. Some require Microsoft Word documents, while others will only accept résumés formatted in HTML, PDF, or plain ASCII text. Many employers now find candidates' résumés through search engines, which makes it more important for candidates to use appropriate keywords when writing a résumé. Larger employers use electronic résumé processing systems to handle high volumes of résumés. Job ads may guide applicants to email a résumé to a company or visit its website and submit an electronic résumé.

Evaluation of Résumé

Different résumé development agencies provide résumé evaluation services wherein they analyse the résumé and recommend required changes. Candidates are free to either do those changes themselves or may take help of the agency itself. Some career fields include a special section listing the lifelong works of the author: for computer-related fields, the softography; for musicians and composers, the discography; for actors, a filmography. Keeping résumés online has become increasingly common for people in professions that benefit from the multimedia and rich detail that are offered by an HTML résumé, such as actors, photographers, graphic designers, developers, dancers, etc. Job seekers are finding an ever increasing demand to have an electronic version of their résumé available to employers and professionals who use Internet recruiting. Online résumé distribution services have emerged to allow job seekers to distribute their résumés to numerous employers of their choice through email. An advantage to online résumés is the significant cost saving compared to traditional hiring methods. In the United States, the Employment Management Association has included Internet advertising in its cost-per-hire surveys for several years. In 1997, for example, it reported that the average cost-per-hire for a print ad was $3,295, while the average cost-per-hire for the Internet was $377. This in turn has cut costs for many growing organizations, as well as saving time and energy in recruitment. Prior to the development of résumés in electronic formats, employers would have to sort through massive stacks of paper to find suitable candidates without any way of filtering out the poor candidates. Employers are now in a position to set search parameters in their database of résumés to decrease the number of résumés which must be reviewed in detail in finding the ideal candidate.

Finally, the Internet is empowering new technologies to be used on résumés, such as video résumés—particularly popular for multimedia job seekers. Other technology that is emerging is résumés that are graphic-enabled.

❑❑❑

40

Importance of an Informational Interview

Requesting an Informational Interview

Informal networking remains one of the best sources of job details and opportunities. It paves a way to probe a specific career field and supports you in choosing the right career path. And while you get advice on where you might find the best fit, you are expanding your network of contacts for future reference. You can easily develop an impressive network. Following is the list for ideas of potential sources for contacts:

- Professors, friends, relatives and former employers—or any professionals these people recommend.
- Local Work Source office.
- Members of professional associations.
- People in the information business-resource centre directors or librarians.
- Human Resource directors, public relations officials, or public information specialists.
- Community service agencies or area Chambers of Commerce.

In addition, there is an alumni which can be approached through an appointment with your school's career consultant or through your alumni association's web site. After identifying probable contacts, ask for an informational interview. All these sources can be contacted by phone, mail or email:

❖ By Phone

Before connecting the call, it is important to prepare an outline of what would you like to say on the phone. This will help you in satisfying all your queries related to the job. You may also appear organized and professional. If you are calling someone by referral, make sure you state that person's name early in the phone call. Also say right away that you only need 20 to 30 minutes of their time. You should mention that you would prefer to meet in person instead of just by telephone. When arranging an appointment by phone, the following points are to be kept in mind:

- Offer a personal introduction.
- Identify your aim for seeking an appointment.
- Decide a mutually convenient time.

❖ By Letter

If you are planning to contact via letter, it is important to follow proper business format. It is also important to double check for spelling, grammar and typing mistakes. Conclude the letter with a specific action – such as a statement that you will call on a specific date to arrange a meeting time convenient for the person. This is usually a week after you mail the letter. Just in case of calling for an interview, a letter requesting an appointment should consist of:

- A personal introduction.
- Your purpose for seeking the appointment.

Piloting the Informational Interview

Before the Interview:

- Study as much as you can regarding the organization.
- Write down the questions that you want to ask.
- If possible, study something about the person you are interviewing.
- Dress professionally.
- Bring multiple copies of your résumé (distribute these only if they are requested).
- Arrive 5 to 10 minutes before your turn.

During the Interview:

- Reiterate your purpose for speaking with this particular person.
- You are the interviewer, so be ready to start the conversation.
- Keep to the original time request of 20 to 30 minutes.
- Seek referrals to other individuals in the field or in related firms.
- Let the person you are interviewing bring up the discussion of specific job vacancies.

After the Interview:

- Send a thank you note and keep the person you have interviewed posted on your job hunting progress.
- Assess your form of interviewing. Use what you have learned for when you conduct your job interviews.
- Assess all the information you received.

What to Ask

Prepare a list of queries you would like to be solved about a career field or organization. Your questions will extract the maximum information if you use open-ended questions to engross your contact in conversation. Following are some of the sample questions to help you prepare for your interview.

Questions about the Career Field

- What sorts of positions are most often found in your career field?
- What abilities will I need to perform responsibilities (such as organizing, supervising, writing)?
- What specific talents do I need to do the job (academic, experiential or others)?
- What training or education is needed to perform duty?
- What would you change if you could?
- What is an entry-level position in this field?
- What chances for advancement do employees have?

- What are substitute methods to gain entrance to this field (e.g., part-time, mid-career change, volunteer work or other kinds of training)?
- What is the future of this field in terms of new and expanding opportunities?
- What other information may be supportive (e.g., critique of résumé, job seeking tactics, names of other professionals in the field)?

Questions about the Firm

- What are the short- and long-term aims of the organization, such as growth, new products or services, and expansion of facilities?
- What is the philosophy of the organization and the kinds of training programmes available?
- Do you have descriptions of the various positions you have held between your entry-level and present job?
- Could you define your current job (as defined in the job description as well as what is done beyond the job description)?
- What is the usual career path from entry-level to top management?

Informational interviewing is an impactful instrument in your approach to career planning. It can be one of your most significant tactics in collecting information and establishing contacts as you begin or continue to build plans for the future. Like all other components of career planning, informational interviewing needs planning and focus on your part. Consider each informational interview a valuable step towards starting your career.

Tailoring Job Interview for Specific Audiences

While travelling overseas, have you ever noticed how native people welcome your attempts to communicate in their language? While no one may take you for a local, people encourage you when you show respect for their culture and point of view. Likewise, if you're interviewing for a job these days, there are good chances that you'll be meeting with people in multiple areas of the company. While they don't expect you to be an expert in every area, employers do like it when you can 'speak their language'. Of course you don't have to learn all the buzzwords, but the more you can speak to their specific functional areas, the better chance you'll have of landing that job. Successful people always maintain a good relation with their audience and tailor their communication to appeal to those they're addressing. All you require to do in your interview answers is relate your experience to other areas in the company. Following are some of the approaches:

Sell Your Experience

Keeping in view the co-operative nature of the workplace, few things happen without a cross-functional effort. When a functional lead quizzes you, impress his/her how you have been successful in working with their area to attain an objective. For instance, if you're in conversation with a finance person and you are in marketing, discuss how finance played a big role in the development of the project strategies. Finance may have driven the revenue targets, the budget and ROI. It's important to discuss how you worked together with finance, not simply asked them for numbers. Highlighting how you worked together will let them know that you value their input and recognize what's important to them.

Relate Your Results

The expression 'No man is an island' works more than ever these days. Your success is reliant on teamwork and the performance of others within or out of your group. You're in sales, meeting with someone in manufacturing. Let them know how manufacturing contributed to your success. For instance, by minimizing costs, you as a sales representative were able to underprice your competitors.

Show How Their Area Helped You

Communicate them how their functional area (irrespective of what it is) shaped your career. This will make them feel good about what they do, and more importantly, they will feel good about you. If you are in operations, and you're being interviewed by HR, discuss how HR in your previous firm helped you with management skills, which positioned you for promotion.

Understand Their Challenges

The idea of an interesting person is someone who's interested in me. The same is true for the interviewer: If you present interest in their job, they'll find you likeable. Quiz them about their goals for the area. They will relish clarifying on that and the challenges they have in achieving that goal.

Tell Them You Admire Them

Communicate that you believe in working as a team and view all achievements as a win for the company. As almost every firm has team-building activities, quiz about theirs and what they do to bring different functional areas together. In this very competitive environment, you can miss good opportunity if you don't appear to be coming from a collaborative mindset. It is also important to prove in your interviews that you see the wide picture and vows the contributions of all departments.

❑❑❑

41

Tips to Undertake Group Discussion and Interviews

We understand that an interview refers to a one-on-one discussion, and the Group Discussion refers to many-on-many discussion. If the many-on-many discussion is not managed to make it one-on-many, the results are less than stellar. On some occasions, the group discussion is moderated (for instance, in news programmes on television) and sometimes it is not moderated (for instance, in jury deliberations, in class team projects).

The benefit of a moderated group discussion is that the participant knows what to discuss and when to interject and put forth their views - obviously, when prompted by the moderator. The challenge to the participant is to know the subject matter thoroughly and be articulate in responding to questions and arguments. One must become a good listener and be able to support or rebut the arguments from others in the group. Thus, preparation for the participant involves learning the subject matter, anticipating as many questions and arguments as possible. Acquiring content knowledge is a necessary step but not a sufficient step. You have to practice applying the knowledge to various real and imaginary situations/scenarios. It is the both the acquisition and application of knowledge that is supreme.

Group discussions, that are not moderated, face additional problems. In addition to the knowledge of subject, one also has to be cautious about what to say and when to say it. In such a discussion, just as in jury deliberations, a quasi-leader (that is, moderator) usually emerges as the discussion progresses. So what are the appropriate rules of engagement in a group discussion? Since only one participant may emerge as the group leader as the discussion progresses, some of the guidelines that may be helpful to all participants are given below.

Directions for Group Discussions That Are Not Moderated:

- Be focused on the topic. You need to share the responsibility to make the group productive to a greater extent. Do not go off on tangents, and if someone else does, make an attempt to bring the discussion back on track.
- Open your mouth only when you have something useful to say. Try avoiding the waste of 'air time'. Just because one talks a lot does not mean one contributes a lot. Strike a careful balance between the quantity and quality of talk. Your speaking contribution should either move the discussion forward or change the direction of the discussion.
- Listen, Listen Listen. Do not get caught up with what great things you can say. Recognize other people's contribution, before you expect them to recognize yours. Continuity of discussion, and thus progress, can be achieved only when participants 'build on' other's contributions. It does not mean you have to accept whatever other participants say — you need to challenge that by all means, if necessary — but listen first.
- One at a time, please! Only one person should talk at a time, while all others should listen.
- Side meetings should be avoided. Do not talk to others, out loud or whispering softly, when someone is talking to the group. If you have questions or comments, try asking the group.
- Be polite but confident. No matter how right you think you are, others' ideas at least deserve due consideration. Never utter phrases such as: 'You are wrong!' 'That is so stupid!' 'Dumbest thing I have ever heard!' - Even when you are 100% sure. Present an alternative way of looking at the situation and let the group support the right path forward.
- Try to lead the group, but with all good motives. Sure, being unofficially recognized by your peers in the group shows your leadership qualities. Only one person can become that. Typically, the group consensus emerges over time. One does not need to be labelled a leader explicitly to acquire and discharge

the expected role. Most often, the group, through its behaviour, implicitly grants the role without verbally articulating it.

- Leader, DON'T push it. Always note, the group had elected you, whether implicitly or explicitly, the leader/moderator. The group expects you to be fair to all participants while making progress. Give everybody a fair chance to speak. Do not let anyone dominate the air time. Make people speak who are quiet and make it a dynamic group.

Since you would be in an environment where you would be assessed, you will be observed for not only what you contribute but also on how and when you contribute.

❑❑❑

42

Stages in Developing Personality

Personality refers to a complex hypothetical construct that has been explained in different ways. In daily life we may came across many people, It's the fact that we wonder why some people are quiet and passive while others are loud and aggressive. The word personality is best to describe it. Personality is set of qualities that distinguish an individual from other on manners, attitude, behaviour and qualities that make the person standout from the crowd. Personality is defined by both outlook or appearance of an individual as well as by ways an individual reacts and interacts with others. It also highlights the psychological system of a person.

Personality factors depend on genetics along with the stimuli in which an individual organism is born and raised up. The physical appearance, bone structure stature, gender and energy level are ruled by heredity material or genetic variation. Personality Traits such as shyness, fear, aggression, actions and attitude are also attributed to genetics and DNA heredity. The culture in which a person is brought up, social circles such as friend, and family colleagues etc. are some of environmental factors that influence personality of an individual. Moreover there are many other researchers conducted by various scientist over personality traits and variation of personality from one individual to another for example when an employ goes for an interview and a company wants a perfect applicant for their work they will not look at his practical skills but also the overall personality factor plays an important role. Therefore, there are multiple theories on the personality explained such as big five, psychodynamic, personality measures which talks about the personality of individual discussing each and minute factors about the personality of an individual.

Psychodynamic Approach

'Our unconscious mind determines our Behaviour'.

This personality development theory was proposed by Sigmund Freud. He opined that an individual's personality is developed in the first 6–7 years of his/her childhood.

As per this theory, our personality has three components.

1. ***Consciousness:*** The memories and moments about which we are aware off.
2. ***Unconsciousness:*** About which we have no idea/unawareness.
3. ***Preconscious:*** Where the memories are in our unconscious but can be brought into our consciousness with a small effort.

Personality Interview: Questions and Answers

Usually the most difficult questions in a job interview are those that are linked to personality.

Even though you think you have a great and well-suited personality for the job, you might think you're being put on-the-spot or falling into a trap because you don't know what type of answer the interviewer would expect from you.

You never know when you'll be faced with such questions associated with personality traits.

Some interviewers ask such questions and some don't. Industry-wise, such questions are used across the board – so it doesn't matter if you're on a healthcare job search or being interviewed for a sales position. These questions can arise and they can be downright puzzling.

❖ Tips to Answer Personality Questions Associated with Job Interviews

A few examples of personality questions that could come up on an interview are as follows.

No doubt, a variety of questions can be asked, so there is no way to anticipate every one:

- ***Talk about your weaknesses***

  This one is bit difficult to answer as no one wants to talk about the negative aspect when they appear for a job interview.

  Mentioning your flaws can only exhibit the employer why not to hire you. So what do you do? The best thing to do in this situation is to turn your weakness into strength. A possible answer could focus on an area where you have more to learn about a particular skill. As long as it isn't a compulsory qualification for the job (one where you require a great level of proficiency) you can say:

  'I haven't had enough experience with electronic health records and desire to learn more about them. I believe this position will offer me an excellent opportunity to enhance my skills in this area'.

- ***Tell me about a time you tried an innovative approach. What was the result?***

  Any 'tell me about a time' questions can be very disconcerting.

  You definitely don't want to be sitting there with your eyes to the ceiling and your mouth hanging open as you think through your brain for an old experience to mention. You also don't want to say, 'I can't think of any'. The best thing you can do with these types of questions is to prepare for the interview by reviewing your work history. Understand each and every point you mention in your resume and letters of recommendations or any employment history or old communications you have.

  Pen down specifically interesting projects you worked on and ponder about positive experiences you can allude to.

  You might not have the best answer to this question, but having an answer is the key. Put forth a positive story, even if the situation didn't end in a complete success. You can always say,

  'It was the first time I tried that approach and I learned a lot from the process. The result was short of what I was aiming for, but I learned why this was the outcome and was able to adjust for it the next time'.

No doubt, having a completely successful tale to tell is also an excellent response.

The more you can quantify your results, the better (e.g. 'The Company saved $30,000 by implementing my new procedure'.).

- ***'What books have you read lately?'***

  This is truly a question of a personal choice.

  This may seem to be disconnected to the job, but the good news is you can make it relate to the job. When conducting your job search, it is important to keep up with your industry. What publications should you be reading as a career-driven person of your industry? Are there manuals, magazines, books, online sites, and blogs? If you're prepared, you have the perfect opportunity to show you've been keeping your skills and industry-knowledge up-to-date. This is also a great way to save yourself if you aren't a pleasure reader. If you do enjoy reading, you should discuss these books, as long as they seem appropriate. Discussing titles that show your appreciation of literature (even popular fiction) or your desire to learn (non-fiction) are fine. For instance, if you truly are reading a biography about Benjamin Franklin, then be sure to say so. If you aren't, never try to lie to 'look good' because you never know what the interviewer would perceive about your personality.

  Maybe he or she is a Ben Franklin enthusiast! You need to be always honest.

  Preparing for the interview is the key to having something to say and being honest about it.

Other questions connected to personality can include:

1. How do you overcome conflicts in general?
2. Who has had the most influence on your life and why?
3. What would you want to work as if you were not in this field?

4. Talk about some of your strengths as sales person?
5. Do you think yourself to be a perfectionist?
6. What is your communication style?
7. How do you manage difficult personalities?
8. How do you manage conflicts in the workplace?
9. How would you describe and rate your leadership style and skills?
10. Where do you want to be in five years from now?

❑❑❑

43

Handling Interview Questions Related to Personality

As discussed, a personality interview doesn't have to be scary if you prepare well in advance by reviewing your own history and researching your industry, the company and available position.

Don't be too nervous thinking of potential questions. Not every interviewer will use them. With those who do, just be calm, confident, and stay on the positive side. Employers know that personality questions and personality tests are difficult for those in the interview seat. Often they want to see if you can keep your composure. They also use them to eliminate anyone who would disclose something strange or extremely negative about their history, attitude or methods.

Never worry about things you do not have control on. Always be ready to bring any topic around to show how you can contribute positively to the company.

Questions related to personality job interview give you the opportunity to show how you are the perfect fit for the position! Lynn Mattoon is a Content Editor & Career Writer for HealthCareJobSite.com, SalesHeads.com and other Beyond.com career communities. You can follow her on Twitter at Beyond Careers.

❑❑❑

44

Important Tips to Learn for the IAS Personality Test

When you face an IAS interview, a candidate's confidence, personality and understanding of the things and happenings all around the society and the world as a whole are evaluated. The interview round is quite subjective in nature rather than objective. Questions asked to a candidate by the interview board are well framed to judge the candidate's overall personality. Thus, answers to the questions should be provided taking into consideration all possible views. A candidate should always try to take a balanced approach while giving answers to any questions.

A. The UPSC interview board is extremely experienced and knowledgeable. In case, a candidate is not aware of something about which he/she was asked, it is always right to admit the non-awareness with humility.

B. A candidate should understand the question properly and then proceed to answer. If the question put in front of him/her is not clear enough, the candidate should politely ask for clarity. You should understand that it is not the factual knowledge but your views which are on test in the interview.

C. You should always maintain interview etiquette. You should be honest, polite, convincing and modest. The candidate's focus on the issue on which he/she has been asked is given more importance. Therefore, arrogance, rigidity, flicking round the issue will not work and is advised to avoid these.

D. A candidate's confidence and honesty are also evaluated apart from his/her general awareness about the world. It is always alright to say no if the candidate has not heard of something instead of beating around the bush.

E. While preparing for the interview, group discussion is a must. Though personality is a life time asset yet, efforts can be made to eliminate major deficiencies and polishing of thoughts and opinions of the candidate.

F. You can participate in the mock interviews held by friends, seniors or teachers. You can also approach some IAS coaching centres where you get right directions by experienced teachers. In the institutes, group discussions can help candidates polish up their views and opinions related to different topics.

❑❑❑

45

Benefits of Preparing Some Important Topics for IAS Interview

The IAS Interview is the most important stage of the IAS exam as the probability of selection is very high and the candidate should put in all the efforts for the interview to get in the final list of selected candidates.

Preparing topics well in advance is always going to be a good idea to anticipate and estimate about the questions which can be asked in the Interview. The IAS Interview is one of the hardest nut to crack because it can make or break within half an hour or so. Hence, hard preparation is needed for the candidates. This article includes different aspects of the topics the candidates should prepare for.

Important Interview Topics/Issues

❖ Vienna Convention

- What do you mean by Vienna Convention?
- How is it important?
- Up to what extent, it affects the International Interaction and relation?
- What are the effects of Vienna Conventions on India-US relations?

❖ Judicial Activism

- What do you mean by Judicial Activism?
- Give instances of Judicial Activism.
- Is Judicial Activism disrupting the Fine Balance between the Executive and Judiciary as sought by our Founding Fathers?
- How do you justify Judicial Activism?

❖ State Reorganization Commission

- Constitution and State Reorganization
- State Autonomy and the State Reorganization
- Need for the Second State Reorganization Commission

❖ Lok Sabha Elections

- Details of the machinery indulged in Lok Sabha Elections
- Comparing Two Party System and Multi-Party System
- Latest Increase in the Expenditure Limit in the Lok Sabha Elections will lead to the dominance of money power in the Election Process.
- The current state of Information Technology and the Inception of online Voting

❖ Whistleblower

- Who is called a Whistleblower?
- Need of Whistleblower
- The Legislative ways to ensure protection of Whistleblower in India.

❑❑❑

46

Model IAS Interview Questions

Some possible questions that appear generally in the UPSC Interview are as follows:

- Some primary questions are usually asked on the basis of your bio-data; about your career choices and why precisely you want to opt for the civil services.
- To initiate the discussion, the IAS interview board usually ask an aspirant to briefly describe about himself/herself.
- Some questions may be related to your name. You may be asked about the meaning of your name, surname and the motive for carrying a long surname or surnames if anybody has.
- Make sure to study some important events on the year or the date of your birth. A majority of the Interview questions are mainly from what you have filled in your form including your subjects, hobbies, service preferences, etc. Thus, you should think of interview as a test of logic and presentation and awareness rather than a pure subject awareness.
- You should have full understanding of the hobby that you mention on your bio-data. Questions are asked on the reason for your following such a hobby.
- You should remain aware about the hot topics of the present world. You will be confronted with some burning issues and will be judged with your opinions regarding the same. Thus you need to have a good knowledge on the current topics as well as an analytical mind to answer the interview board.
- You are asked questions related to your profession/professions if you have any. If you are a doctor, then you might be asked questions on any ongoing health issues. If you have an economy background, then you might be asked questions on the current economic scenario. The board may also ask you about the

applicability of your current profession in the civil services. So, you should be well prepared on all the possible questions relating your past and present careers.

- You may also face some situational questions in the interview. For instance, the interviewers may ask give you a situation and ask how you will deal with the same. For example, if you were the Collector/SP of Ajmer, Rajasthan, what would you do after the bomb blast in the city? So, you are supposed to develop an analytical and foreseen thinker mind to face the IAS interview.
- Questions may be from any subject. Thus, you need to have a deep knowledge and good analytical view to clear the hurdle of interview.

❑❑❑

47

Developing the Best Techniques to Prepare for IAS Interview

Usually, IAS Interviews are conducted in the month of March and April. IAS interview is often considered as the toughest stage of the three tier examination process, and it appears to be even tougher when we start developing fear for it. So, the first step in preparing IAS interview is to stop having any fear for it. The no fear approach need not however be artificially cultivated rather we need to appreciate that after having endured and overcome the tortuous mains exam, a candidate comes to acquire enough knowledge, acumen and insight to deal with the complex and intriguing problems of public life, with a fair degree of maturity and tact. So, anybody who has prepared well for the mains exam, thoroughly evaluated and processed the concepts and applications presented by different disciplines within the fold of the syllabus of the IAS exam hardly needs to fear the attitude and knowledge testing questions put forth during the interview, which is regarded as the toughest part of the interview.

Now, once you have confidence about the attitude and knowledge testing part of the interview, what remains is just working over your presentation, composure and demeanour. These three components are however again a part of your overall personality, which you have got over a period of time and practically no significant improvements are possible with respect to these aspects in a short period of time after the mains exam.

Therefore, the vital advice at this point is just to 'be yourself', without making an attempt to bring in so many changes in a short time period, which would ultimately bring more harm than good. The only thing which you can and should do at this point of time is to polish your existing acquired skills in some ways. Some important things you can consider are as follows:

1. Keep updated with the current events and keep practicing your analytical skills and insightful abilities by trying to see them in perspective, which mainly implies drawing useful meanings out of a whole lot of happenings which take place in the public domain.
2. Attend mock interviews which will expose you to live settings. The feedback can help you understand and learn from the mistakes you are likely to commit on the actual interview day. This exercise is especially useful to shine your presentation, composure and demeanour.
3. Work on things like your resume and hobbies so that you could justify your past choices and interests and put forth an inspired and focused impression.

Finally, have full faith in yourself, which will drive you back to yourself till the very end with all confidence and poise.

❑❑❑

48

Best Test of the Personality of an IAS Interview Candidate

The purpose of Union Public Service Commission interviews is to evaluate the personal suitability of a candidate for the service he/she has applied for. An interview board interviews the candidates. The interview aims to assess the mental calibre of a candidate, not just his intellectual qualities but also his social traits and interests in current affairs.

The method of the interview is a natural one. It comprises of a direct and purposive conversation, which aims to disclose the mental qualities of the candidate. The Interview preparation process is continuous. All knowledge a candidate has acquired during his academic as well as his personal life contribute in the preparation of the interview. This involves a wide reading of books, journals, magazines and newspapers etc. The interview test is not meant for judging the candidates academic knowledge only, rather it is a test of the candidate's overall personality. That is why appropriately it is called a personality test rather than an interview. Besides the academic preparation, the candidate should also put stress on the ways to improve his/her conversational skills with right body language and expressions. Candidates can participate in group discussions with friends and seniors to understand each other' mistakes and thus can work on them to bring improvement and present themselves in front of the interview board.

The candidates have to fill the examination form with the required columns of his/her interests and hobbies. At the time of interview, the interview board maintains the information provided by the candidate and they do ask some questions from the candidate's bio-data.

So, candidates should be ready to face questions which may arise from their bio-data. Besides, the interview board tests the knowledge and grasp of candidate on the optional subjects which he/she has passed during the mains examination.

Thus, an overall preparation of the academic and personal front of the candidate is needed to face the IAS interview.

❑❑❑

49

Learning Tips to Sharpen Your Skills for IAS Interview

Looking for a new job? Wishing to show the world your capabilities? Searching for ways to sharpen your skills? If your answer is in affirmative to all these questions, then you are at the right place. This article will serve you with exactly what you are looking for. In the world of competition it's very difficult to get the desired job easily. Also as the adage goes-'Many apply but few are hired', is pretty true. However getting hired is only possible when an individual has a set of unique skills that makes him stand out from the ordinary crowd and bestows a chance to grab the golden opportunity awaiting him. Some guidelines that will help you build your interview skills and get your dream job are as follows:

Remove fear and replace it with your confidence

No doubt, job interview is something that is very difficult for all job seekers, but overcoming your nervousness and your fear is something imperative and urgent. You must enhance the level of your confidence instead as it will help you in expressing your views and ideas, thus overcoming problems in communication.

Convince yourself first if you want to convince others

'The post that you are applying is perfect for you and you are perfect for the post as well', should be the feeling coming all the time in your mind. This can happen only when you have full confidence over your abilities and skills and you have no room for doubts as how, why, etc. Thus, if you convince yourself in a suitable way that you are the most suited for this job, it's not a big thing to convince yourself.

Work on your appearance for your better future!

Your dressing is something that reflects a lot about your personality, your background, your mind-set, your approach towards life and it is also considered to be the first thing to make the impact without telling anything. You need to dress professionally for an interview, which means wear well-fitted skirt suit or a trouser suit. Besides, to get a whole corporate look, wear small ponytail, subtle makeup, shiny shoes and no extravagant accessories. That's all.

Think before answering a question

Think properly before you answer to any questions. This will help leave a good impression as it will show them that you are a good listener and do not lack patience and will definitely show the same with your work. In addition, taking time to answer a question shows your professionalism as against shooting out the very first thought coming to your mind. Also be crisp, brief and honest while answering the questions.

Thus, these are the skills that you need to work on and master them before you move for the interview. You should consider that as a golden opportunity in real terms.

❑❑❑

50

Significance of Stress Management in Interview

Stress Management

This book intends to aid you recognize and understand anxiety and nervousness which is a common phenomenon during presentations or interviews. This is as also called performance anxiety. The guide also provides strategies to help you minimize any detrimental effects and offers a number of further sources of help and advice.

❖ What is performance anxiety?

Majority of people become nervous while speaking publicly, either in a room, conference delegates or an interview panel. This is occasionally called performance anxiety. Performance anxiety, however, is not necessarily harmful; a slightly increased anxiety level can motivate you to do the work needed so that you are effectively prepared for the event: it can make you more alert and energized. But, if your anxiety levels and nerves become too great, difficulties can happen, which may weaken your ability to prepare effectively for and perform during the event.

❖ What causes it?

Performance anxiety and nerves can occur due to the following factors:

- thinking about past performance during presentations or interviews;
- how you will compete with your friends or other students;
- any negative concerns if you don't do as well as you would like;
- other's reaction towards your work.
- Lack of preparation as indicated by:

- hastily writing the presentation at the last minute;
- not preparing practicing your speech;
- not thinking in advance about the kinds of questions the interviewer might ask.

It is really tough to chalk out any specific cause, you may just be aware that you typically experience nerves or anxiety at the prospect of an interview.

❖ What are the consequences of being nervous?

Some specific reactions occur automatically when you experience nerves, anxiety or stress about any event. If you think about a time when you were interviewed or made a presentation, you may come to know that you reacted in some of the following ways:

- your voice shivered;
- you had sweaty palms;
- you felt shortness of breath;
- your heartbeat speeded;
- you had butterflies or an upset stomach;
- you felt a generalized feeling of fear.

These very factors crop up due to production of hormones and lead us to fight or escape from situations that are dangerous or threatening. This is called the fight or flight response; your body is alert, ready for action and is preparing itself to cope with the situation. Once the threatening event is over, your body will gradually return to normal. While this process is framed to help you during potentially threatening situations, it can pose difficulties, particularly if your level of anxiety is too great and/or it occurs for a long time period.

❖ What are the signs of performance anxiety?

There are ample of symptoms that appear when you are nervous about any event. They could begin just before your interview, hours or days before it, or even at the moment you find out about it. Signs can even remain throughout your interview. The signs could include negative thoughts such as 'I'll never manage it'; 'It will be a disaster'; 'I'm no good at this'. Having thoughts of this kind can distort your perception of the event and create a cycle whereby the more negatively you think about it, the more stressed and anxious you become, which in turn can increase your negative thoughts about it and so on. Being negative thinker can also have a big impact on your feelings; you may be aware of feeling scared about the event or you may feel generally irritable but not be sure why. You may also witness behavioural variations, such as putting off thinking about and planning for the interview, or alternatively being unable to stop thinking about and planning for it. You may also witness physical changes, such as having headaches, changes in your appetite or developing sleeping difficulties.

❖ Tactics to help you deal with performance anxiety

The tactics outlined below provide some simple steps that will control your level of performance anxiety. However, to ensure they have a positive effect, you need to be active in implementing them prior to and during the event.

1. ***Cultivate positive thinking and visualization skills:*** As already previously, being a negative thinker means that you may be facing performance anxiety. It is helpful, therefore, to be aware of some of the usual negative thought patterns so that you can try to replace them with positive patterns. Try to become aware if you are having negative thoughts and, if so, think of a positive replacement for them (you could consider asking your friends to help you with this). It may also be useful to visualize yourself successfully completing the task. Imagine yourself coming out of the interview or presentation and moving on to other things in your life beyond the anxiety provoking experience. Plan a treat or social event post interview irrespective of the outcome. Using these processes will help you to keep a sense of perspective about the event and stop things from spiralling out of control. Make a habit to focus on your present and future actions instead of thinking about past happenings.

2. ***Plan and rehearse your presentation wisely:*** Your anxiety level can be minimized to a great level by planning and practicing for your interview carefully. After planning, you will feel more confident and presentable. The better prepared you are and the more you know your material, the more likely you will be to recall it when you are feeling nervous or stressed. When you are rehearsing for your interview or presentation, picture yourself as if you are in front of your audience/interview panel and rehearse out loud. If possible, rehearse in front of some friends who could provide you a constructive feedback about your verbal and non-verbal communication, and your time-keeping. Record an audio or video tape of yourself if you do not feel comfortable with friends. You can then listen or watch the tape and provide your own feedback. Identify at least five positive things about your skills, as well as areas for further development. Preparing for questions during an interview may also help to lower your anxiety levels. Read over your presentation notes or application form critically to identify areas of possible weakness and prepare positive answers. Your friends and staff in the University may be able to help you with this. During the interview, do not rush to answer the question. Try to give yourself some time to think before responding. Practical advice and guidance on how to prepare and deliver powerful presentations are available from the Student Learning Centre, College House. A number of free study guides are available, and there are individual consultations for one-to-one advice. For guidance on interview technique, the Careers Service provides a number of guides, videos, one-to-one consultations and workshops.

3. ***Trace your anxieties:*** It is important to trace the situations which increase your anxiety levels and eliminate them by making a plan to be successful. Imagine the interview and write down the aspects which cause you to feel particularly anxious, and then identify something you could do in advance which would help to prevent this from occurring. For instance, if you are worried about using equipment, make sure that you

practice using it before the event. On the other hand, if you are concerned that a weakness will be highlighted, frame a positive response to this in advance.

4. ***Take care of yourself:*** Being physically and emotionally sound will help to limit your anxiety levels so that you feel relaxed when you are under stress. The following tactics are recommended:
   - Have a well-balanced diet which limits alcohol, caffeine and sugary foods.
   - Take between six to eight hours sleep per night.
   - Try to exercise regularly as this uses up nervous energy and relaxes muscles.
   - Take time for yourself for participating in a sport or hobby.
   - Practice taking control of your breathing. Concentrate on breathing out to a slow count of four; the breathing in will take care of itself.

❖ On the day of the event

1. ***Assume that you will feel some nerves or anxiety:*** Before the interview, assume that you will have some nerves or anxiety. This will help you to prepare your mind to cope with pressure. So, it is important to not eliminate your nerves totally, but aim to keep them manageable. You can also expect to feel nervous particularly at the start of the interview or presentation and it is likely that you may feel shaky or possibly your voice will tremble. If this does happen, change to a slower pace, breathe more deeply and expect that the tremble/shakiness will go away. People do expect to see some nerves at the outset. Give yourself some time to settle into the interview and then guide yourself properly as the event progresses. Nerves can make you speed up or slow you down on the day. If you are having note cards in a presentation, you will find it helpful to put reminders to yourself to check the time and to think about whether you need to slow down or speed up.
2. ***Be confident:*** don't jump to conclusions about people's reactions: Try and wipe out any negative feeling from your

mind and think positive. Tell yourself you can do it and try not to jump to conclusions about how people appear to be reacting to you. Some people may look stern or uninterested, when they are actually just trying very hard to understand what you are saying.

3. ***Be relaxed physically:*** Try the breathing exercise discussed previously. You may also find it helpful to do a relaxation exercise to release muscular tension in places such as the neck and shoulders. Take some deep breaths, aim to increase the distance between your shoulders and your ears. This will help to lengthen your muscles and relieve tension.
4. ***Be careful about what you eat and drink:*** Do not take eatables high in sugar, alcohol or caffeine as these can make you feel jittery. It can be better to have a warm rather than cold drink just before the interview. Cold drinks tend to constrict the vocal chords and may increase the likelihood of your voice shivering.
5. ***Prepare tactics in case you feel overwhelmed:*** Do something that will break your frozen state. Try and change your posture or focus your gaze just above peoples' eyes for a few seconds which may help you to collect your thoughts. Even then you are not able to think anything, you may need to ask for a short amount of time to concentrate because you have lost your train of thought through nerves. People are usually supportive and will think more positively if they see you trying to gain composure.
6. ***Praise yourself for a job done***
   - Do not forget to reward yourself afterwards for a job done irrespective of the performance, and then do something which you enjoy as a special treat.
   - Think what can you contribute in eliminating the same performance anxiety in a friend.
   - Friends are usually the first people we turn to when we are under stress. Often, very simple things can help.
   - Try to make your friend more professional and confident by developing positive thinking about the situation.

Encourage them to do the best that they can and to accept that they are not a failure if they do not do as well as they would have liked.

- ❖ Help them to prepare and practice their interview tactics. Give them constructive feedback which highlights some good aspects of their techniques along with identifying areas that could be improved.
- ❖ If you will be present during his/her presentation, give your friend some encouragement and feedback during the session. Smile, show interest or ask a question.
- ❖ Make sure to meet them after the interview and support them irrespective of their performance.
- ❖ Plan something enjoyable to do afterwards to celebrate a job done.
- ❖ Motivate them to follow the strategies outlined in the guide and to look out for further support if these tactics are not working.
- ❖ Don't take them to the pub beforehand – it rarely has the desired effect!

Stress Management in IAS Exam

It is well-known fact that the civil services exam is one of the toughest nuts to crack nation-wide. The UPSC candidates cope with lot of issues along with the mostly ignored issue called 'stress'. A majority of aspirants move away from their families for the preparation and take up accommodations which provide little comfort. Some don't know how to cook and completely dependent on the mess food or street food. They put in 15 to 18 hours of hard work because of the pressure. The dearth of sleep, unhealthy food and mental pressure cause a lot of physical and mental issues. Stress and anxiety are common among the youth, but they are not considered a problem until they become monster to only haunt them. So, if you are stressed, deal with it now and deal with it in the right manner. Following are some of the tips:

- ***Train your brain to be quiet:*** Meditation can be of great help. Meditating for just 10 minutes a day can do wonders for your brain. Meditation helps you deal better with a lot of things in life. It significantly helps in eliminating the random negative thoughts that occupy your mind and contribute to stress and anxiety.

- ***Get proper rest:*** It is important to get proper sleep (7–8 hours) for healthy body and mind. Chronic sleep deprivation can really strain your nerves and reduce your cognitive abilities, reduce your IQ and also your concentration power. Follow a simple night-time routine to help you unwind better. Setting a bedtime alarm can be very helpful. Also, make the environment around you conducive to sleep.
- ***Keep yourself happy:*** Being happy is very vital for being positive. Happiness is a habit and not an effect as most people would like to think. Nothing causes a person to be happy, you are happy because you want to be. So, you must never stop wanting to be happy. Try to find and do things that make you happy each day. A positive mindset is the key.
- ***Think of the big picture:*** Do not put your mind in trivial things and forget your goal. It is important to give yourself some time and think about positives an not negatives to take smart decisions.
- ***Eat a balanced diet:*** Have a well-balanced diet rich in vitamins, nutrients, etc. to keep your stress levels down. A hormone called cortisol is responsible for causing stress in your system. Magnesium helps reduce the cortisol levels. Food such as nuts, leafy greens, berries and raw cocoa are high in magnesium content. Have a low-sugar and high-protein diet. Do not skip meals and snack on healthy foods.
- ***Intake a lot of water:*** It is important to take sufficient water to remain healthy. Lack of water causes a havoc in your system if you are working under pressure.
- ***Find a hobby:*** Art keeps you occupied in a meaningful way and also helps you de-stress. So, find a hobby and stick to it.

Challenge your body, let your mind take the backseat: Physical workout is really good for the brain, as it releases the feel-good hormones like endorphins. It also helps improve your brain's cognitive performance and problem solving abilities. It also helps boost long-term memory. You can choose to do yoga, cardio exercises or something simpler like a run in your neighbourhood or brisk walking.

- ***Read more (watch less TV):*** Reading makes the mind relax. It not only entertains but exercises your brain and makes you a much knowledgeable person with the ability of striking up a conversation with anyone anywhere.

The way an individual handles the stress can be a deciding factors for his/her success or failure. Performance is a combination of intelligence and your state of mind. While you keep acquiring more knowledge, but if your state of mind is not right it is of no avail. So, handling stress is very important. The best way to avoid being nervous is to think beyond the task that needs to be accomplished. If you think too much about the task, you will end up stressing so instead look at yourself beyond the process. This will amazingly calm your mind. During the course of your preparation keep your mind as stress free as you can. Take corrective steps to avoid any such problems that might be hampering your preparation. You should work towards having sound mind and body which is also a prerequisite for your IAS preparation. So, make every attempt to make a plan to be successful. Be calm, composed, cheerful and jolly. Do your best and leave the rest.

❑❑❑

51

IAS Interview: A Concluding Overview

The Interview is the last and final stage held after the results of mains are declared in the process of selection for the civil services. It happens in many cases that a candidate clears preliminary and main exams but fails at this stage due to various factors. It is really very important to start preparation for interview along with the written test. According to UPSC, the goal behind this final stage is to assess the personality and suitability of the candidate.

The interview is the test of overall character and skills and not a specialized knowledge. The aim of this is to assess the social qualities of a person and his personality as suited to a career in the civil services. Scoring well in the IAS interview needs a package of knowledge, smartness and other qualities that are detailed in this complete guide to the IAS interview. Being good in English is not mandatory to score high marks. In addition, you also don't need to remember all facts and figures to score high marks.

In contrast, following are the points considered:

- You should have constructive thoughts
- You should have fresh and unique thoughts
- There must be integrity
- Honesty plays an important role
- Firmness is another important thing
- Having patience is necessary

An aspirant should be true to himself/herself and do not fake his personality to impress the Board. The more natural you are, the more chances you have of getting selected.

As interview is to assess the mental qualities of candidates, it is important for a candidate to prepare well on questions related to bio-data and current event of national and international importance.

For preparing for the stage of interview, a candidate has to go through wide range of books, journals, magazines and at least two newspapers.

An aspirant should have good conversational skills with the right pronunciation.

It is also important for the aspirant to assess his/her strengths and weaknesses and make a conscious effort to play on his strengths.

Following are some of the helpful tips to fare well in the interview stage:

- Body language should be positive
- Answers should be clear and confident
- Candidate should remain calm and composed
- Short explanation with important points
- Do not be argumentative.

Elementary Topics to Prepare for Interview

It is very important to fill the form with right mindset and do not included false information regarding your hobbies and interests in it. Because majority of questions arise from that form itself. As the Board has very experienced members, they will test your patience by picking up your loopholes. So, prepare in advance for anything that you think is important.

- Name meaning and origin of the name. Any personality associated with the name.
- Hometown – for what it is famous for, geography and history of the place, origin of the name.
- Important dates – importance of birth (birthday), important days and dates.
- Sports – in-depth knowledge of sport you mentioned in the form, famous players associated with them, rules of the game and other important details.
- Details regarding your hobbies and interests should be studied in deep.

- Educational background – questions can come from subject and stream of graduation, and place from where the candidate completed 10th /12th/graduation.

Apart from the above questions or subjects, following are some questions who demand extreme care while answering:

- Why do you want to join civil services?
- What will you do if do not get selected?
- Why should we select you?

❑❑❑